CHIEF TECHNOLOGY OFFICER

Defining the **Responsibilities** of the Senior Technical Executive

DR. ROGER D SMITH

Modelbenders Press

Modelbenders Press books may be purchased for business and promotional use or for special sales. For information please contact the publisher.

The following are trademarks of Modelbenders LLC:
"5 Patterns of the CTO" and the hexagonal graphic associated with it, The CTO Spectrum, The Alignment Axe, and the Game Augmented Model of Decision Making.

PRINTED IN THE UNITED STATES OF AMERICA

Visit our web site at www.modelbenders.com

Designed by Adina Cucicov at Flamingo Designs

The Library of Congress has cataloged the paperback edition as follows:

Smith, Roger
Chief Technology Officer: Defining the Responsibilities of the Senior Technical Executive.
    Roger Smith. – 1st ed.
    1. Technology Management   2. Executive Leadership
    3. Business Organization   I. Roger Smith   II. Title

ISBN-13: 978-0-9823040-4-4
ISBN-10: 0-9823040-4-8

Table of Contents

FOREWORD

The significant role that technology plays in major business decisions has created the need for executives who understand technology and recognize its profitable application to products, services, and processes. The ability to turn new ideas, materials, and services into products has become a differentiator between industry leaders and those who fall behind. This force is so powerful that is has even changed the structure and direction of mighty General Electric. Jeffery Immelt and Scott Donnelly have made significant changes to Jack Welch's old company, many of which center on leveraging new technologies and fostering innovation.

Like GE, many companies have addressed this need through the appointment of a technology executive like the Chief Technology Officer (CTO), Vice President of Technology, Director of R&D, or Technical Director. This person's responsibilities include:

- Monitoring new technologies and assessing their potential to create new products or improve existing ones
- Directing R&D investments to projects that can add value to the company
- Providing reliable technical assessments of potential mergers and acquisitions
- Explaining company products and growth strategies to the trade media
- Participating in government and professional groups in ways that empower the company.

This book explores the role of the technology executive in three parts. The first focuses on technology leadership positions, their emergence, its growing importance, and the transformations that the position brings to these companies. The second explores the CTO's relationship to innovation in R&D laboratories and business units across the company. This ties the book to the wealth of innovation literature that has recently been so popular. The third provides industry-specific profiles of CTOs and their unique responsibilities in manufacturing, defense, and government.

As companies have grown more technically sophisticated the need for an executive leader who can deal with this new field as a strategic resource has increased. The Director of R&D and the relatively new CIO initially received the brunt of this work. However, in the past, the Director of R&D has been more accustomed to managing scientists to explore new concepts; not managing diverse resources toward financial and market advantages for the company. The CIO is focused on the internal application of IT and building partnerships with other companies. Since neither of these fits the new demands of the company, the Chief Technology Officer position has become the executive-level host for these responsibilities. People like Scott Donnelly, GE Senior Vice President for Global Technology; Padmasree Warrior, CTO of Motorola and more recently Cisco; and Darren McKnight, Senior VP of SAIC are leading the empowerment of this position.

At GE, the CTO is focused on the technology behind lighting, turbines, medical equipment, and numerous other business areas. At Motorola, the CTO is concerned with wireless communications and the computer chips that improve communication performance. At ALCOA, the focus is the composition and process for working metals. Only at

IT companies is there confusion on separating the CTO from the CIO. These companies often find it difficult to determine when IT is an internal business function and when it is a product for a customer.

Though technology is permeating every aspect of business, very little has been written about the roles and responsibilities of the CTO. The dotcom explosion created an entire publishing industry focused on IT and the CIO. The growing need for competitive advantage and productivity based on new technologies will create a similar strong market for information about the CTO and similar technology management positions. This book is the first really useful work to focus on this point.

The book brings together the experiences of practicing CTOs, the research of academics, and the strategies of technology-based companies. The companies will continue to custom design the position, and this book will equip them with best practices in industry, academic concepts, and the experiences of others who have gone before them.

This book began as a research project whose results were initially published in *Research-Technology Management*, the journal of the Industrial Research Institute (IRI). The role of the CTO is a core issue at IRI, which includes technology executives from ConocoPhillips, Corning, Lockheed Martin, Boeing, SAIC, Dow Chemical, Air Products, International Paper, Lucent India, DaimlerChrysler, and many of the other Fortune 200 companies.

Each chapter in the book was originally written as a stand-alone article for a journal, trade magazine, or web site. As a result, though they all follow a common theme, they can be read as a series of independent works.

Intended Audience

Industry

This book targets senior technology executives with titles like CTO, VP of Technology, Director of R&D, and Technical Director. It will attract the attentions of the executives who must select a technology leader, the managers who work with them, and the young technologists/managers who aspire to these positions.

The book will also find an audience among CIOs who are technology executives themselves; though with a very specific focus. The book will assist them in separating their responsibilities from those of the CTO, and perhaps convince the executive committee to create a CTO position if the demand exists.

Academia

The academic market includes business schools that offer Management of Technology programs and the students who are searching for resources to help them excel in these programs. My research led me to Edward Roberts at the MIT Sloan School of Management and Fred Betz at the University of Maryland's Robert H. Smith School of Business. Both of these professors have provided leadership in structuring Management of Technology programs and have written textbooks to support those programs.

Market Need

The publishing industry generates hundreds of books on management topics every year and often targets them at specific management positions. However, material speaking directly to the CTO is surprisingly scarce even though the position has been part of companies like ALCOA, GE, Motorola, and IBM for decades. A search of Amazon.com provides an interesting picture of management books targeted at specific executive positions.

Amazon.com Search Results

CEO	3,989
Board of Directors	1,649
CIO	801
CFO	312
CTO	2

The extreme shortage of titles on the CTO position illustrates that a working CTO has almost no resources available from which to build his or her expertise in the position.

1

EMERGENCE OF THE CTO

The position of Chief Technology Officer is relatively new, emerging from the position of R&D laboratory director in the 1980s (Parker, 2002). Therefore, the definition of what a CTO is and how this person should contribute to an organization varies widely. In some cases, this variation is driven either by the unique business needs or by the evolutionary path that created the position within a specific company. In other cases, the variation is a result of a misunderstanding of the role of the CTO or of simply mimicking the role used in other companies.

When asked what a CTO is, Nathan Myhrvold, the former CTO of Microsoft and head of its massive research organization, replied,

> *"Hell if I know. You know, when Bill [Gates] and I were discussing my taking this job, at one point he said, Okay, what are the great examples of successful CTO's. After about five minutes we decided that, well, there must be some, but we didn't have on the tip of our tongues exactly who was a great CTO, because many of the people who actually were great CTO's didn't have that title, and at least some of the people who have that title arguably aren't great at it. My job at Microsoft is to worry about technology in the future. If you want to have a great future you have to start thinking about it in the present, because when the future's here you won't have the time."* (Brockman, not dated)

Though the position is new, it is being widely used in many different industries. A Google search on the term "Chief Technology Officer" returns 392,000 hits, most of which are corporate announcements of the appointment of a new CTO. These announcements span the breadth of industries, including:

- IT, computer, and research organizations such as SAS, Intel, and the Fraunhofer Institute
- Heavy production companies such as Siemens, ALCOA, and ChevronTexaco
- Service providers such as Federal Express, National Association of Convenience Stores, and Hewitt Associates
- Government agencies such as the CIA, Air Force Research Laboratory, and the City of Washington D.C.

Clearly each of these industries has a very different business model, customer base, internal structure, and culture. It is unlikely, if not impossible, for one definition to meet the needs of all of these organizations.

Given such a large number of CTOs in service, we would expect a solid foundation of journal, magazine, and trade book publications on the subject. Surprisingly, what we actually found from an archival database search on the term and its three-letter abbreviation were fewer than 20 published journal articles in the last 10 years (Smith, 2003). It is no wonder that the position is poorly understood and unevenly applied. CTOs are not publishing their activities and academics are not researching the position.

With such a vague idea of what a CTO should do, one would expect many people in the position to be "winging it" and their superiors to be evaluating them based on trial-and-error. CTOs must define for themselves what they should do, and their bosses must largely accept that definition without a basis for comparison and evaluation. In this article we will examine some of the prototypical forms of the CTO and their roles at various junctures in the corporate lifecycle. The goal is to identify the most effective style of CTO for a company at a specific stage in their development.

CTO Categories, Skills, and Focus

The CTO position is occupied by people with diverse backgrounds, as is common to other executive positions like the CEO, COO, and CIO. Since the CTO position is often confused or interchangeable with the CIO position, and since both are relatively new to the executive ranks, it should be no surprise that the skill and background of the CTO is at least as diverse as that found in the CIO position.

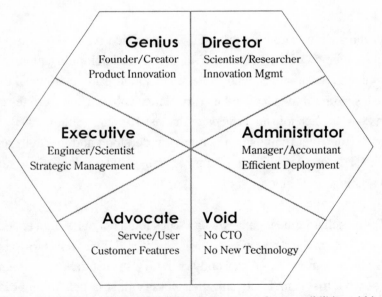

Figure 1.1 CTO positions exhibit five distinct sets of responsibilities within the organization requiring different skills and unique foci.

In studying the backgrounds, responsibilities, and missions of a number of CTOs, we identified several distinct categories of CTO (Figure 1.1). These categories are driven by unique stages in business evolution and by the needs of specific industries. Clearly separating these categories and associating them with a business phase or industry sheds considerable light on references to the CTO in the trade press and corporate statements.

Genius

We are in the midst of technology revolutions in computers, information services, biotechnology, nanotechnology, medical products, and pharmaceuticals. The seeds of these industries are often traced back to a few innovators with the personal drive, talent, and opportunity to explore the unknown. People like Steve Wozniak of Apple Computer and Sergey Brin of Google have become the Thomas Edisons of this generation. They demonstrate the power of an idea championed and largely matured by a single person. These are the archetypes of the Genius CTO category.

When a company, technology, or industry is in its formative stages, the CTO is often a technical genius about whom larger-than-life legends will be told by later generations. He or she (192 of the first 200 CTOs returned by a Google search are men) may be pulling together a number of available concepts and products in a new way; as Wozniak did with the first Apple computer. Or the CTO may be commercializing a new technology that has emerged from a university or commercial laboratory, as Sergey Brin did with the Google search engine (Boorstein and Watson, 2003).

The Genius CTO is usually skilled at creating something new, possessing vision and confidence, and exploiting a unique opportunity.

This ability or skill is essential to a company that is emerging from the garage or presenting its concepts before a panel of venture capitalists. Some technologies can be formed and matured largely through the efforts of a single exceptional person. When this is possible, the Genius CTO is the type of person that an emerging company needs.

However, the Genius CTO may have poor skills for managing teams of people, administering processes across an organization, or working with executives on a long-term strategy. Like Winston Churchill, their skills may be essential at a critical point in history, but they are not necessarily the best person to fill the position once the crisis is over and the company has moved on to larger problems, processes, and structures.

Administrator

In many cases, the CTO must guard the organization's budgets from overspending on technology products, services, and project labor. The CTO must be prepared to negotiate with outside vendors and service providers to insure that the company is receiving the resources it needs, but at the same time, not overpaying for them. Government offices that rely on technology-based products and services to create new products for civil, military, and intelligence applications fall into this category. Without such a person, the government buyers and users of technology are not in a position to effectively separate marketing claims for technical facts. The office then finds itself at the mercy of the vendor representatives and their claims for their products.

Jeffery Pound, the CTO of the Air Force Research Laboratory, is one example of an Administrator CTO. Pound has been involved in two major endeavors along these lines. The first was a deal in which he negotiated a favorable licensing agreement with Microsoft that saved AFRL $9.6 million in fees. Equipped with an understanding of the laboratory's technical needs, Pound was able to identify the type and number of products that were essential and eliminate wasted licenses. He has also been working with vendors and developers to identify new ways to increase the security of the lab's networks without seriously impacting their performance (Jones, 2000). These projects require an appreciation and understanding of both the technical aspects and the financial impacts of technical issues in the laboratory.

Director

As a company grows large enough to sustain and benefit from a research and development laboratory, future CTOs can emerge from that organization. He or she may be a leading scientist or researcher who has shown a talent for organization, handling exceptional people, and envisioning the future. If such a person is willing to give up direct, hands-on research in order to create an environment in which others are enabled to do outstanding and valuable work, then they may become the Director of R&D and a future CTO. In some companies, the title CTO is a direct substitute for Director of R&D. The organizational implications behind this are that the labs must make a direct contribution to the company's financial performance and competitive position. To encourage, enable, or enforce this, the Director is pulled into the executive ranks and retitled the CTO. In other companies, the CTO is an additional position designed to bridge the gap between the company's strategies and its research activities.

Pat Gelsinger, the first CTO of Intel Corporation, is an excellent example of this category. Gelsinger lead Intel Labs, Intel Research, and the Intel Architecture Group. He is extremely well versed in the technical aspects of Intel's products. He is focused on converting research and laboratory work into profitable products for the company. To quote from the Gelsinger's Intel bio, *"As CTO, he coordinates Intel's longer-term research efforts and helps ensure consistency from Intel's emerging computing, networking and communications products and technologies."* (Intel web site)

Nathan Myhrvold also exhibited the Director CTO style when he created Microsoft Research. He recognized that the world's leading software developer needed to pioneer new technologies to be integrated into its world-dominating products. It needed collaborative relationships with academic researchers and a conduit for engaging those people on problems of interest to Microsoft. The result was a world-class organization that is now investigating speech and vision interfaces, machine translation, spam filtering, new Internet technologies, multimedia, and dozens of other technologies that will become part of their future products.

In creating and managing such a research lab, the CTO must be able to separate ideas with great potential from those that are challenging and exciting, but lack the ability to become or contribute to great products. The actual Director of R&D will be more focused on sponsoring important research projects, while the CTO matches research ideas with the strategic plans of the company and its broader capabilities to move a new technology into the marketplace. He or she must consider whether great technology can be manufactured efficiently, priced competitively, delivered to the customer, and whether it will be a product that a customer will embrace.

Executive

Large corporations that use technology as a key component of their products or services have been the most aggressive at applying the CTO to their innovation process. Companies like GE Medical, AL-COA, Corning, ChevronTexaco, and IBM have all become known for their use of a CTO to assist in guiding strategic decisions and managing the innovation process. The Executive CTO is a businessperson who measures innovation, research, and experimentation by the contribution it makes the company's revenues and future competitive advantage.

This person's background may be just as scientific and research focused as the R&D Director described earlier, but their current focus and purpose are different. They are an integrated part of the executive staff and are relied upon just as the CFO, COO, and CIO are to assist in directing and managing the business.

Dr. Malcolm O'Neill, CTO of Lockheed Martin, is an excellent example of an Executive CTO. He is responsible for the company's research projects, but is also directly tied to the company's engineering, program management, and mission execution (National Academies web site). His role includes consideration of operations beyond the research labs. He must foster the exchange of ideas and technology between the research, manufacturing, service, and contracting operations of a 130,000 employee global company.

Advocate

Rob Carter, CTO of FedEx, has received numerous awards from the IT community for transforming the IT infrastructure of the world's leading overnight shipper. Carter and FedEx realized that over 70%

of their customers used electronic transactions in shipping packages. They recognized that improving the IT experience for the customers could drastically improve the efficiency, profitability, and market share of the company. This implementation also made dramatic contributions to FedEx's expansion into international markets (Gotcher, 2000).

Carter represents the Advocate CTO who is generally focused on the customer's experience of and interfaces with the company. This type of CTO is most often found in retail, service, and government organizations. These CTOs do not usually direct the creation of technology, but rather select and combine the best products for their specific business capabilities.

President Bush's plan to make all government services available electronically and to create an electronic conduit between every government office and their constituents, has challenged government CIOs and CTOs to build a modern, customer-centric computer infrastructure. Together, these two executives must identify, evaluate, deploy, and maintain IT systems that meet their customers' needs.

Organizations of this type may assign these responsibilities to the CIO since he or she has traditionally been the acquirer and integrator of IT technologies. This practice has contributed to the blurring of the responsibilities of the CIO and CTO. Most writers maintain that the CIO should be focused on the internal IT needs of the organization, while the CTO should be focused on technology as it applies to products, customers, revenues, and competitive positioning in the market (Spiers, 2001). When the technology involved is strictly IT, it is feasible for this work to be combined with the CIO's traditional internal IT work. However, for companies where the technology is pharmacological research, new rocket fuels, and computer chip manufacturing, this combination would not even be considered.

Void

Finally, there are the companies that intentionally decide that they do not need a CTO. Many of these have stable sustaining businesses that incorporate very little new technology and do so only after the industry has already defined a stable solution. However, companies that are leading change in "non-technical" businesses are probably encountering issues for which a CTO would be very useful.

One could argue that a grocery chain does not need a CTO to improve sales of produce, meats, and canned goods. But, in-store computerization and automation argue otherwise. The Point of Sale (POS) terminals in most grocery stores are advanced computing systems. To the degree that they collect accurate data, manage inventory, and allow a store to predict future sales, these POS systems can be seen as part of the CIOs mission. But, when they are specifically designed to improve the speed at which customers are served or the systems are strategically located to provide information in the aisles, they are becoming an application of technology aimed at the customer.

Recognizing that service lines form at the deli counter, Stop and Shop grocery has installed tablet PCs in the aisles to allow customers to place deli orders to be picked up later in their shopping trip. These types of systems are competitive tools just as fresh produce, baked goods, and meats are. They allow the store to differentiate itself from competitors, attracting additional revenue. Computerized control of lighting, refrigeration, in-store advertising, bakery and deli cooking systems, and a host of others are part of the store's competitive advantage (Patton, 2002).

These represent a domain of the business for which a CTO can be used to identify the best solutions and implement them in the most efficient manner. Some of these responsibilities can be handled by the CIO; as has been done in other industries. But that is a misfit of function and mission. Reaching in-store customers and convincing them that the store should be their shopping site of choice requires a different focus, mindset, and talent base from those traditionally found in the CIO's organization.

The CTO and associated staff are not necessary for every business, but they are probably not being used in many businesses that could benefit from their contributions. Just as modern corporations have developed the need for a CFO, and more recently a CIO, the continued evolution of business, technology, and society will broaden the industrial base for which a CTO is needed.

Examples of the duties of each of the five CTO patterns.

Pattern	Duties and Activities
Genius	Personally involved in the creation of new technology and its application to company products and services. Uses personal technical talent to direct and motivate the technical staff.
Administrator	Guardian or watchdog over the organization's selection and use of vendor technologies. Expertise with technologies is used to accurately evaluate vendor proposals and claims for their products.

Director	Manager of corporate research projects and investments. Handles the business aspects of a portfolio of different technologies that the company is pursuing.
Executive	Strategic leader working with company executives to identify important technical trends in the future and how these will impact the company and the industry.
Advocate	Focused on the applications of technology to improve the experience of the customer. Leverages technology to create a competitive advantage for the company through its relationship with customers.
Void	Companies that could benefit from a technology leader, but who do not understand how such a position could be applied.

Matching the CTO to the Business Phase

Like all other positions, the skill set needed for the CTO varies based on the type of business, industry, and maturity of the company. The person who was perfect for leading the company during its early phases may be completely wrong for the same position when the company is expanding. This is especially true when trying to organize innovation across multiple locations, in different lines of business, and with a larger employee base. The types of CTOs we have described can be found in companies at all stages of their lifecycle. But, there are noticeable relationships between the type of CTO selected and the phase that a business has reached in its evolution (Figure 1.2).

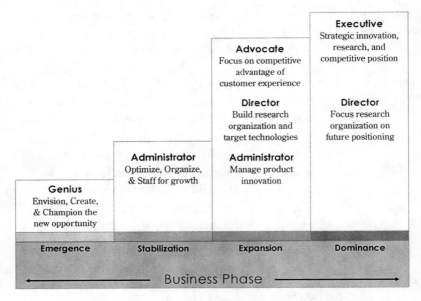

Figure 1.2 Matching the CTO to the Business Phase

Emergence

The Genius is most likely to hold the CTO position when the company is just emerging. He or she may be one of the original founders and may have been responsible for the key technologies or products that made the company a viable business. Such has been the case within many dot.com and IT companies in recent years. The Genius CTO earned a place in the executive ranks, but was not equipped or inclined to take a role in management, accounting, marketing, or production. But, his or her enthusiasm for the product or service provides the energy and motivation that make the company a unique place to work or that motivates the staff to put in extended hours without immediate financial reward.

The Genius CTO will share in strategic decisions and the financial rewards afforded to the CEO, CFO, COO, and CIO of the business. The position places technical innovation on an equal footing with other business functions in guiding the company and influencing its direction from the very beginning.

Stabilization

After a company has successfully emerged, it will find that some of the ad hoc and chaotic processes for creating new technology and products do not extend well to larger groups. As more people are added to the company, there is a much greater diversity in capabilities, perspective, and understanding of the mission. As this occurs, the technical leader and visionary will find it necessary to apply more time and energy toward unifying people and projects. The Genius may find it difficult to shift his or her attention from purely technical tasks toward management and communication. This leads to the need for a more Administrative CTO that excels at working within a diverse environment of people, organizational structures, and business issues.

Since most companies do not remain in the emerging category, this transition is inevitable within the professional life of the original Genius CTO. When this occurs, the CTO must either change his or her operating approach or find a way to share responsibility with a more administratively skilled partner. The Genius CTO may gravitate toward the head of a small R&D center within the company; if such a unit exists. The Genius CTO may also become a "Director of Product Innovation" or some similar role. Other companies anoint the CTO as a Fellow, create a Chief Innovation Officer, or establish a small research team for the person to lead. Each of these requires great tack on the part of the company and humility on the part of the founding CTO.

Expansion

As the company expands and becomes a major player in the industry, it may find itself with a number of competing candidates for the
CTO position. The Administrator and Genius CTOs that had previously filled the position will still be available. But a Director of R&D and
an engineering executive can emerge as potential competitors for the
CTO position.

An Administrator CTO may recognize that the resources dedicated
to new products have grown significantly. From this perspective, the
CTO role seems to call for additional management and organization.
Therefore it is natural for the Administrator CTO to oppose releasing
the position and argue that administrative and organizational expertise
is needed now more than ever.

The Director of R&D may perceive that innovations from the laboratory are having a significant impact on the company's new products and
the ability to generate profits or maintain a competitive advantage. This
perspective calls for more attention to research and an executive role
for someone intimately familiar with and successful in that domain.

If technology forms a strong connection between the company and
its customers, as in the case of FedEx described earlier, a representative of those customers may argue that the CTO position needs to be
focused on improving the customer experience. Hence, the Advocate
CTO becomes another competitor for the position.

Just as there was competition for the CTO position as the company
moved from Emergence to Stabilization, it will face even more competition as Stabilization gives way to Expansion. The selection of the CTO

will lie with the CEO and an Executive Committee. They will have to decide which direction holds the most promise. Ideally, their decision will be based on an analysis of the future prospects of the company and the most profitable aspects of their chosen market.

Dominance

Companies like GE, IBM, Microsoft, and Siemens have arrived at a position in which they dominate multiple markets. Their focus is no longer on growing their traditional market because they have already achieved a dominating position—such as Microsoft's practical monopoly of the desktop operating environment. Instead, these companies look for ways to either create new markets or leverage their expertise into adjacent markets.

Creating new markets often requires a strong contribution from the R&D labs to provide a differentiated capability upon which to build. In this case, a dominant company will rely upon the Director CTO to elicit innovation from researchers that can be turned into products. The motivation is less science and technology for its own sake, and more science and technology as the linchpin of a new product or service. Microsoft exhibited this approach when they determined to move into the videogame console market. They had no expertise in developing hardware as most of their previous products were software. They began from scratch to create a new kind of gaming console that could compete against industry leaders Nintendo and Sony, and redefine the game console at the same time. This battle is still raging, but Microsoft has been instrumental in dislodging Nintendo from their second place position. They are still struggling for an advantage over Sony's Playstation, which possesses the strongest list of game titles, largest installed base, and most productive game studios.

IBM on the other hand, has seen the strong demand for e-business services and has leveraged their expertise in both hardware and service support to become a major IT consultant and solution provider. Their WebSphere products and services have made them a strong competitor against more established IT consultants like Accenture and PricewaterhouseCoopers (PwC). IBM recognized that computers, software, and the Internet were creating a strong connection between customers and major companies, however Accenture and PwC had traditionally focused on internal IT projects. Therefore, IBM moved into the new business area before the consulting companies could completely dominate it. Now that IBM has purchased PwC, it can focus the strengths of both companies against the remaining IT consulting firms.

The CTO of a dominant company must be involved in strategies to move into new markets or to adapt and invade adjacent markets. The Genius and Administrator CTOs do not usually possess the best perspective and experience-base necessary to work in this area. It requires someone with technical expertise who is also used to working hand-in-hand at the CEO, COO, and CFO level on very large, sometimes long-term, strategies. The CTO will be required to provide a perspective on technology that is targeted at achieving a competitive advantage and generating attractive profits. Specific technical details of products and components are not useful at this level. Neither are the skills of managing teams, overseeing production, and optimizing schedules; the most effective capabilities for the CTO of a dominant company. These companies need a CTO who sees technology as a means of achieving a larger business objective.

Conclusion

Twenty years is a very short period in which to evolve a new executive position. In this time we have seen the rapid emergence and adoption of both the CIO and CTO positions. The urgent need for information systems and common ways of applying them have driven the maturing process for the CIO much faster than that of the CTO. Since the role of the CTO is much more dependent upon the type and phase of the business, it is difficult to set a common definition for the position. We have identified several common categories of CTOs as they are found in major industries and have discussed the alignment of these categories with specific business phases. These categories and alignments are not exhaustive, but they are very useful in guiding new CTOs and assisting them in anticipating conflicts and changes that will arise in the position.

What is the CTO's Role?

Genius CTO: *"The greatest CTOs that I know are the ones that take architecture seriously. Architecture guides the constraints and shows what's important and what isn't. It bridges the creativity of the engineer to something that can achieve a high impact for the company."*

Greg Papadopoulos, CTO, Sun Microsystems

Director CTO: *"The CTO nurtures and cultivates new ideas and innovation in both the technologies and the processes by which we build and design large complex aerospace systems. The CTO must focus the enterprise or company so it can be responsive to new technology and capitalize on it."*

David Whelan, CTO, Boeing Space and Communications

Administrator CTO: *"Every basic business process must work. That takes 80 percent of our time—replacing awful, ugly work process. Each one of the agencies must operate in an efficient way."*

Suzanne Peck, CTO, District of Columbia

Executive CTO: *"The CTO's key tasks are not those of lab director writ large but, rather, of a technical businessperson deeply involved in shaping and implementing overall corporate strategy."*

W.W. Lewis, Sloan Management Review

Advocate CTO: *"You get a B- to C+ grade as a CTO if you solve problems as they come along. If you want an A or a B, you have to teach your people how to prevent those problems in the first place."*

Craig Humphreys, CTO, H-E-B

2

THE CTO IN TRANSITION

The team of people that come together to form a company with a technological foundation will certainly include someone who is a master of the technology, or ambitious to become such a master. This person, treated in the singular here, will experience his or her first transition very early in the process.

A technologist will have mastered a set of skills that allow him or her to manipulate technology effectively. This person will be able to work with the software, electrical, chemical, or biological materials to create a new and useful product. Computer programmers understand the language, operating system, hardware, and development tools that allow them to manipulate symbolic instructions to the computer. Electrical engineers will be able to design and/or construct circuits that can identify images, process signals, or control mechanical devices. As a creator or manipulator, this technologist will derive a degree of satisfaction from this ability, take great pride in it, and often tie his or her personal identity to this set of skills. This deep personal investment in technical skills is an important ingredient in driving a technologist to create a new company or product in the first place. It is one thing that has brought that person into the company of others eager to begin a new venture. It is also the primary source of their value to the group.

An ambitious technologist will be comfortable taking a hands-on role in the creation of the product and in making decisions that shape it. He or she will probably be accustomed to leading others through the force of technical expertise and possess the ability to demonstrate this when challenges arise. However, as the enterprise grows, its technical base will expand until it exceeds his or her ability to be an expert in every area. As with other leaders, there are four sources of power that the CTO may employ. The first is the expert power that is often the most familiar to the

CTO. He or she is used to leading people by being the best programmer, engineer, or scientist on the team and enjoying the respect and deference that accompanies that position. An extension of expert power is referent power in which the people being led accept that the CTO has power based on a respected reputation and/or the desire of the members of the team to be accepted and acknowledged by the CTO. This power emanates from those being led. A group grants representative power to a person that they have selected as their ambassador or leader. Political leaders are chosen and empowered in this way. Legitimate power comes from the chain of command. It is considered legitimate because the company grants it in order to achieve their objectives. Members of that company accept the legitimacy of the chain of command as part of their employment. Finally, there is coercive power; a form that is often the least familiar to the CTO. Coercive power stems from the CTO's ability to punish employees or grant rewards (Newell, 2002). To be an effective leader, the CTO must move beyond expert power and learn to employ the other forms of power effectively.

The technical expert is an invaluable ingredient in a new company. Technical skills are often the showcase of the company's capabilities, and the person who has been knighted as the CTO of the company will be required to perform feats of expertise in front of investors, the news media, and industry professionals. This is the first transition—from "doer" to "advertisement for doing". As a person, the CTO must be comfortable in the spotlight and have a certain flare that radiates confidence. If he or she does not possess this style, it can be taught; as it was at Symantec in the early years. Ron Moritz, CTO of Symantec, was an extremely proficient security professional, but largely unknown to the industry press. Symantec President, Roberto Medrano, created the marketing campaign that made Moritz available to the trade press, conferences, and media events. This was all designed to create an in-house, world recognized expert in the field. In Moritz's words, *"Experts in this industry are like politicians—they are made, nurtured, and coached"* (Aspatore, 2002). This transition is one of the first and smallest that are driven by the needs of the company. Many technologists drive their own careers based on their skills, interests, and personal ambitions. However, when they become an officer of the company and a marquee personality that can influence its future, they relinquish some degree of personal choice of direction and accept corporate direction to meet corporate needs.

While the start-up company is building its foundation, the CTO will switch back and forth between "doing" and "advertisement for doing". This two-headed image is the very beginning of the transition that the CTO will face throughout the transformation of the company.

This transformation, and those that follow, may be called for by the nature of the business. However, it is not absolutely necessary that the technologist or CTO change himself to fit the company's needs. Many technologists choose to remain with their original skill set and image. In this situation, the company must turn to someone else to meet their expanding needs. When a technologist chooses not to be molded by the needs of the company, such a choice is almost synonymous with choosing not to be the CTO. However, it is also possible that the path is too difficult for the technologist to navigate. There are limits on personal growth and company growth. More established companies transition very slowly. In this case, the individual employees find themselves growing at a faster rate than the company can take advantage of. Under these conditions, individuals move from one job to another more challenging position.

However, when the company is growing faster than the individual can grow, then the opposite occurs. The company must move on to a more appropriately skilled person. Just as the growing individual left a hole for the company to fill when he or she moved to a new position; in a fast growing business, the company's need to move forward can leave a hole in the career of the individual that has to be filled by another company. Figure 2.1 illustrates this reversal of the growth rates.

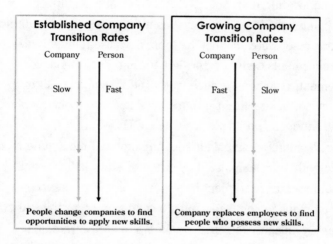

Figure 2.1 Effects of disparate personal and business growth rates.

Managing Technology

If all goes well, the company will succeed at moving through its start-up phase to become a more stable business that is not on the verge of exhausting its finances. A CTO who has played a significant role in achieving this success, like the other executives and risk-takers in the company, will be rewarded financially and organizationally. Retaining or attaining the CTO position is one such reward, and something that has driven the proliferation of the CTO title among technology companies during the last decade.

As the CTO of a small stable company, the newly expanded technologist will assume responsibility for a much broader set of tasks associated with maintaining, maturing, and managing the product. Using a software company and a computer programmer as our examples through these transitions, we find that the CTO who was once simply a programmer is now being called upon to serve as a software engineer. In addition to creating a software product, he must now also handle issues dealing with requirements definition, design, testing, integration, configuration management, quality assurance, and product support. All of these are necessary to ensure that a product maintains its cohesiveness, functionality, and focus on its purpose. The CTO will find that he or she is spending less time manipulating technology and more time managing technology that is manipulated by others (Figure 2.2). Technical expertise is an essential ingredient in performing this task successfully, but significant management skills must be added in order to be as effective at this newly enlarged job as he or she was as a programmer.

Company Stage	CTO Focus	CTO Resources
Start-up	• Inventing • Productizing	Manipulating Technology Timeline = 6 months Budget = $100,000 Leadership = 10 people
Stabilization	• Software Engineering • Configuration Management • Quality Assurance	Managing Technology Timeline = 1-2 years Budget = $10,000,000 Leadership = 100+ people

Figure 2.2 Comparison of the manipulating and managing phases of the CTO position.

Typically this transition has been very difficult for technologists. They find that it impacts their personal identities and significantly changes the set of things that they have enjoyed doing every day. The transition requires relinquishing behaviors that have been directly responsible for personal successes and to replace them with skills that are much less familiar and less respected by a technical peer group.

Within a larger organization that has survived the start-up phase and achieved stability, the issues of concern to the company and the senior leaders will expand in size and extend outward in time. The CTO who was previously concerned with events occurring in the next six months will find that his or her horizon of interest has extended out to one or two years. This person will need to deal with issues regarding the next generation product and the long-term support of the current product. The budget for operations will no longer be limited to the expenses necessary to fund a development team for six months, but will include balancing funds necessary for all technical operations for the next generation of the product. Finally, directly tied to the expansion from programmer to software engineer, will be the inclusion of a larger team of people. These people will not all have the same set of professional skills, be focused on the same urgent objectives, or practice similar business functions.

Planning Products

In the third phase of the evolution of the CTO, the person transitions from managing multiple technologies to planning the next generation of products and services that will drive the company over the next five years. As the technical seeds that launched the company become mature, the executive team, of which the CTO is a member, must look for ways to maintain their position and sustain their growth. Technology-based companies cannot rest on previous successes and expect to remain healthy. Eventually every technology becomes a commodity that is imitated and sold by a number of vendors. When this occurs, the profit margins are far too small to support the research and innovation necessary to invent new products. Therefore, for a technology-driven company to remain on the leading edge and maintain the source of their competitive advantage, they must constantly push into new territory.

The challenge that Dell Computer is presenting to Hewlett Packard in selling printers is an excellent illustration of this need. HP is driven by its ability to invent new technologies to support its core products and to open new markets with new products. Dell, on the other hand, is a distributor of technology developed by others. They may make minor modifications to the product to improve its usability, but they do not make significant investments in research and invention. Therefore, as the technology that drives HP products is released to the public domain, reverse engineered, or imitated, the company loses some of its competitive advantage. Though HP may have sold 43.6 million printers in 2003, companies that can offer similar products at lower prices, because they do not invest in research, are constantly eroding the low end of their product mix. When such a company partners with a distributor like Dell, it significantly accelerates this erosion. Dell has sufficient penetration to influence customer buying across the computer industry, just as Wal-Mart does across consumer products.

In this environment, HP must carefully plan the release of new products or improvements to existing products. It must transform its product-base every couple of years to maintain a unique position that can justify significant profit margins. Without this forward planning, the company will fall into a price war over commodity products. The most damaging effect of such a price war is that the profit margins will not support the significant research and development that gives HP its edge. The results would be to eliminate HP's R&D resources, stop the progression of printing technology, and reduce HP to the level of a vendor of widely available technologies.

Michael Dell has said, *"The days of engineering-led companies are coming to an end"* (Lohr, 2004). This speaks directly to the career transition of the CTO. The skills that keep HP and others like them in a leadership position are not primarily "engineering" or "technical". They are the ability to plan the future product mix, build partnerships that deliver unique advantage, and create financial instruments to fund the company. The engineer is still at the heart of the company, but perhaps not at the head.

Envisioning the Future

If a company is extremely successful, it will achieve a position of industry dominance. Companies such as GE, IBM, Microsoft, ALCOA, Lockheed Martin, GM, Toyota, Cisco, and hundreds of others have transitioned from a small start-up company to a world leader in their field. This is usually a slow process requiring multiple decades of dedicated effort.

The CTOs of such companies have a very unique set of responsibilities. They are charged with envisioning the future. They must serve as a primary catalyst for extracting, organizing, selling, and applying a vision of the future. The "vision thing" is not their responsibility alone, but they are at the crux of generating the vision and applying it across the company. Pat Gelsinger, the CTO of Intel, is driving his company toward a vision of merged computing and communication (Hari, 2003). He must convince technologists across Intel that the future lies in the unification of those two separate industries and that Intel must reside at the center of that unification.

Recently, many companies have recognized that telephone switching need not be a separate network from their computer data networks. Companies are turning to Voice over Internet Protocol (VoIP) telephones rather than traditional analog lines and corporate switching systems. These devices bring both the computer and the telephone services into a single infrastructure and can significantly reduce the cost of telephone services. Eventually this will lead to the realization that there is no need for a separate desktop device for voice and data communications. Next-generation desktop computers will incorporate the functionality and ease of use of the telephone device. At the heart of this new corporate computing device will be computer processors that Intel hopes will come from its factories.

In this situation, Intel and Gelsinger are looking at the next step in the evolution of two different industries. They are seeing the trends that are moving the world into a new configuration and placing themselves in the best position to capitalize on the future. Notice that Intel is not independently trying to create the merger of computers and communication. Instead, they recognize where businesses, customers, and society are moving, and are attempting to apply their own spin to the future that their customers are creating. In most cases, envisioning is not the creation of a new, unique, original, and personal picture of the future. Instead, it accurately perceives where the world is going over the next 5-10 years, and searches for a way to be part of the future that is already forming. The CTO and the corporation seek to find a unique contribution that they can offer to the new world. They become partners with larger forces, contribute to the progress around them, and reap the benefits of helping move society forward.

A CTO trying to ride the corporate transition from "expansion" to "dominance" may or may not be able to convert his or her talents into those necessary to operate at this level. The CTO of a dominant company is more concerned with products that do not exist, market needs that cannot be met, and profit margins that cannot be measured. This person must be able to move away from a focus on existing customers, established competitors, and specified product lines. He or she must be able to envision competition from new sources outside of the traditional industry.

In the convergence of computers and communication, Intel is striving to be the leader. However, they may find their competition coming from Lucent and Cisco rather than their traditional competitors at AMD and IBM. The convergence may transform the computer just as much as it transforms the telephone. It may become more of a communication device as professionals recognize that they use very little of the available computational power of the machine, but rely on it heavily for telephone calls, email, and document formatting. This type of transformation of the market base is something that the CTO of a dominant company must be able to see coming and must be able to prepare the company for. There is no reason that the imagination and foresight have to come from the single person holding the CTO title, but the

CTO is an essential link in expressing those ideas, giving them credibility, and using them to refocus a corporate entity.

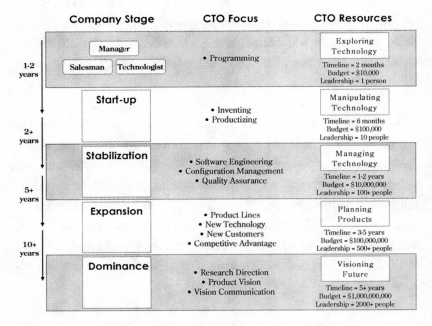

Figure 2.3 Demands of Transition on the CTO

Conclusion

The professional life of the CTO is strongly driven by the state of the company that he or she serves. Early stage companies require much more hands-on expertise with specific technologies. Mid-stage companies need a CTO who can focus on improving existing products and leading teams that can create replacements for those products. Industry dominating companies need a CTO that can place their focus on envisioning the future. This person must be able to find and codify opportunities that exit now or that will arise along the developmental trajectory of the world. Once identified, he or she must be able to influence the corporation to pursue these visions and keep the company on a path to successful innovation; avoiding distractions that diffuse energy and confuse purpose.

Each company and each individual has different growth rates. It is very unlikely that the rate of growth of the company's first CTO will be able to match the growth rate of the company throughout its ascent to higher levels. Traditionally, people have been able to grow and adapt much faster than companies. As a result, we are accustomed to people moving from one job, company, or industry to another. However, in the information age, it is just as likely for companies to grow faster than specific individuals can follow. When this happens, it is the company that must move on to a new employee.

3

THE CTO SPECTRUM OF RESPONSIBILITIES

The responsibilities of a CTO and his or her support organization vary from company to company. Young start-ups typically have a set of technically hands-on tasks for the CTO, while an international conglomerate may need the CTO to deal with the representatives of foreign governments and industry organizations. In spite of this variance, it is important to identify a collection of CTO activities that can generate value for the company.

Advise Value Vision Communicate Manage Innovate Implement

Figure 3.1 The CTO Spectrum

The spectrum of responsibilities of the CTO and the CTO office can serve as motivation and direction for creating a new CTO organization, and can provide a means for evaluating the effectiveness of the CTO and their company. The spectrum provided in this paper spans a wide variety of responsibilities that include corporate strategy, mergers and acquisitions, internal processes, and relationships across the organization. Many of these responsibilities were collected through interviews with numerous CTOs and from trade articles discussing the position. This work is reported in Smith (2003).

Advise

Technology has become an inseparable part of most businesses. In many cases, it is the source of a significant portion of the company's competitive advantage and future revenue generation. As such, the executive leadership of the company must make well-informed decisions regarding future acquisitions, funding decisions, and the application of technologies.

Acquisitions

In the case of an acquisition, the picture painted by the financial numbers is not always an accurate representation of the position of the company. A good deal of its future value stems from the quality and marketability of its technology. The CTO office should have access to the internal expertise necessary to evaluate potential acquisition. Or, when the expertise does not reside in-house, it should be able to locate, contract with, and manage external expertise.

In some cases, a merger or acquisition presents an obvious case for compatibility or improvements in scale. These mergers typically extend the current business base, allowing the resulting company to dominate the current market more strongly. Such mergers require less advice for merging disparate technologies, but can still benefit from such evaluations during the integration phase that follows acquisition. The CTO office is an excellent resource for identifying the best alignment of internal capabilities that hinge on technology values.

When an acquisition is designed to extend the company's capabilities into a new area, that may require detailed and trustworthy valuations of the target company's technology. The CTO office may be commissioned to conduct an investigation into the patents, competitive position, and technical product details of the target company. It is important for the acquirer to have a clear understanding of the value of the target's technology—its ability to beat competitors in the future. The value of the target's technology may be realized through licenses to component developers or system integrators. In this case, the license and relationship with the customer are issues for other members of the acquisition team. But an evaluation of the power of the technology to continue to hold the interest of the customer in the face of competitive products, new inventions, and market trends is the domain of the CTO office.

Funding

At least annually, companies must determine whether to continue funding technology development, and if so, at what level. One part of these decisions is driven by the revenue and profit of the entire company. Another is the immediate need of other functions within the company.

The Directors of research organizations and technology innovators typically create an evaluation board to make these recommendations. Such a board may consist of representatives of each project, external consultants, and internal customer organizations. The CTO office is another source of expertise for these evaluations. Participation in these boards is a two-way relationship. The CTO office participates in order to assist them in making the best decisions. But, the events also provide an information gathering opportunity. These are an excellent source of information about the internal state and activities of the company. Through participation, the CTO office is in a better position to execute many of the functions listed later in this paper.

Henry Chesbrough points out that large labs such as Xerox PARC have always conducted such internal review, but have consistently missed important capabilities or given the green light to projects that provided no financial return (Chesbrough, 2003). He compared this to the process in which a start-up is evaluated by a Venture Capital (VC) firm in order to make a funding decision. The VC typically does not have the staff necessary to perform an in-depth technical analysis. Instead, they rely on the market performance of similar projects to guide their decisions. In the past, this has aided them in financing projects that Xerox PARC declined to support. The participation of the CTO office in these internal reviews is not intended or expected to make the process flawless, but will provide reviewers who are more objective, and who, like a VC, can compare the opportunity to their knowledge of other similar technologies.

Application

In the process of collecting information from across the company, the CTO office will possess a uniquely broad and technically competent view of the capabilities of the entire company. Their encounter with new technologies in labs or application capabilities in a facility will enable them to cross-pollinate the company. They will be able to spread information from one endeavor to another. Innovative new ideas and truly new work will not be isolated to the organizational hole from which it sprang, but will be shared with every other project that the CTO office encounters.

Many companies conduct internal technology conferences specifically to encourage cross-pollination of ideas. These venues allow technologists and managers at all levels to see how business and innovation are done at other sites. These carry the advantage of exposing a large number of diverse people to an unusual combination of new ideas. They have the disadvantage that they are one-shot events that can soon be forgotten in the face of daily responsibilities. The CTO office is a logical group to organize these conferences, manage them, and follow up on the information that is shared.

Key value-added activities that the CTO office can perform related to these conferences are:

1. Organize Conference
2. Identify Best Participants
3. Compile Reference Materials
4. Facilitate Group Discussion
5. Capture Cross-Pollination Intention
6. Distribute Materials
7. Follow-up on Cross-Pollination
8. Provide Resources for Effective Implementation
9. Track and Measure Impacts of Cross-Pollination

Value

As described in the Advise section above, the CTO office can play an important role in determining the value of acquisitions. Investigations by experts who are familiar with state of the art advancements in new technology can make important contributions to the evaluation of a company's technical resources. However, the evaluation of a company is a specialized field whose expertise is not usually resident within every company.

The ability of the CTO office to provide valuation services will vary considerably from one organization to another. If the acquiring company intends to perform multiple acquisitions, then this skill may be something that needs to reside in-house. However, if acquisition is a rare event or maximum objectivity is required, it may be best to hire a valuation consultant.

Experts in technology valuation list a number of factors that should be considered in this process; some are generally applicable and others are unique to a specific situation (Lebbon, 2004).

* Does the corporation own all of the technology?
* Is the technology protected?
* Do other parties have rights to the technology?
* What additional items are required to commercialize the technology?
* Is the technology enduring? For how long?
* Does the technology provide a competitive advantage?
* Are there competing technologies?
* How long will it take to get to market?

Each of these conveys a specific value to the target company. As with most predictive and qualitative measures, the exact number associated with this is an estimate and will vary based upon the characteristics of both the acquirer and the acquiree. Specific technologies have different values stemming from the current and historical business of the company. This fact is clearly exhibited by the number of successful businesses that spun out of Xerox PARC and Hewlett-Packard from the 1970's to the 1990's—creating the strong technology foundation for Silicon Valley. Many of those technologies had less value within their original parent, but once released to seek a different type of customer, they were major businesses in their own right.

Vision

The CTO will be a core part of defining the vision of the company's future. This responsibility has typically been controlled, organized, and even performed largely by the CEO who is responsible to shareholders for the future strength of the company. However, today, no single person can manage all of the details of a major company. The CEO relies upon the CFO for trustworthy financial data, the COO for a smooth, modern operating environment, the CIO for modern IT systems to monitor, report on, and empower the organization—and the CTO for a complete understanding of the technical position of the company to meet the current and future needs of existing and potential customers.

By no means has the CTO inherited ownership of the company's crystal ball for predicting the future of its products or the industry. However, the CTO certainly must peer into those misty depths and identify an important technical feature of the future landscape of the company. As the executive officers and their designated helpers gather around the crystal ball to identify the vision for the future of the company, the CTO must not be a shy or secondary member of the crowd. His or her technical vision is going to make a significant contribution to the capabilities of the company in the future. No longer do most companies conduct business as usual—simply expanding, contracting, or modernizing existing facilities or services. The most successful companies are working hard to identify new business opportunities in the current and adjacent market areas. The company may be transformed over a number of years into something completely different from what it is today.

Companies such as 3M are well known for inventing new products at the very edge of the their current product space. They have moved from sandpaper to tape, electrical equipment, and the most modern computer storage media. Without vision and an appreciation for modern technology, sandpaper looks just like a tool for smoothing wood, metals, and other surfaces. But with vision, sandpaper looks like a thinly coated urface with defined performance specifications. The coating may be grinding particles, tape adhesive, or magnetic data storage—all are coated thin surface products.

The Big Three automotive manufacturers are often seen as dinosaurs that have always made cars and will always limit themselves to making cars. However, each of them long ago recognized that they were in the business of extracting profits from the car-buying customer. Those profits may come from the margins on the sale of a car, the interest points in making a car loan, premium profits on premium options, and revenues from service operations. As soon as one competitor identifies a source of profits, the others must follow suit or trump the move with an even better idea. No company can afford to remain the same if it wants to be a long-term competitor.

In this environment, companies are constantly moving and shifting their business. They are searching for the sweet-spot of profits and attempting to dominate that position for as long as possible before yielding ground to competitors and moving on to the next opportunity. The CTO may not be able to identify sweet-spots like auto financing, but he or she will certainly be able to point the company toward magnetic storage, new materials, environmentally friendly solvents, robotic equipment, and the computerization of factory operations.

Like the CFO, COO, and CIO, the CTO has a unique set of skills and a unique perspective on the problem; a unique view into the crystal ball. Expressing that view, pressing that view, and fighting for attention to that view, is all part of adding value to the company. Failing to satisfy this responsibility hobbles the company and allows a competitor to reach those innovations first and reap the largest rewards.

Communicate

Within most companies there are defined communication networks and media for information on the financial position of the company, legal and personnel issues, and product marketing. However, there is rarely a formal network or vehicle for exchanging technical information and keeping the people who create new products up to date with activities in the rest of the company. The evolution of the modern corporation has led to a structure in which the independence and isolation of each facility, plant, or division extends from its production capabilities into its innovation capabilities. Most manufacturing or service centers contain all of the resources necessary to carry out their operations. Each facility usually has tighter relationships with its stable of suppliers than it does with the other divisions of its own company. As innovation has evolved within these companies, those same barriers have prevented research groups and technical projects from exchanging information across division/plant boundaries.

Since the technologists within a division often share close quarters, there has been little need to enhance communications within that group. But that has also allowed the innovators to work without knowledge of other technology groups across the company. Of course this led to duplication of effort; one group being stuck on a problem that another group had solved, and most importantly, an inability to leverage the work of multiple groups toward a larger objective.

The CTO office bridges the gaps between these islands of innovation. The information that it gathers in the process, must be shared across these barriers and the conferences described above are one excellent tool for accomplishing this. Newsletters, mailing lists, collaborative web sites, chat rooms, and problem-solving bulletin boards are a number of other tools for bridging these gaps.

Each of the media for information exchange achieves two primary goals—(1) the exchange of information and (2) the building of relationships. The first goal presents itself as the primary objective. But, in practice, relationships across the business are much more powerful. The real value of these communication tools is enabling innovators to build their own relationship network. Relationships allow technical experts to make their own contacts, ask their own questions, and build a web of data exchange and solution sharing that is much more powerful than a conference or newsletter.

The most successful thing that the CTO office can do in this area is to stimulate the creation of relationship networks. These relationship networks will replace much of the value of the formal communication tools.

Manage

Where does the culture necessary to foster innovation and communication within a company come from? What keeps it alive? Why is it not regulated, strangled, and marginalized in the face of daily pressures for profits?

To be sure, not all companies are able to create a culture of innovation or collaboration. Even Steve Jobs felt that creating the next generation of Apple computers required isolation in order to protect the culture of innovation from the culture of daily production and maintenance. He established the Macintosh group in a building far away from the Apple campus and regulated access to it.

On the other hand, 3M is stimulating innovation by mandating that employees work on personal projects for a defined percentage of their workday. Encouraging scientists to work on problems that interest them has been one source of valuable inventions like post-it notes and advances in data storage.

In both cases, practices are established with the explicit goal of fostering an environment and a culture that is attractive and conducive to innovation. The CTO encourages, supports, and protects these practices at the executive level. The CTO office is a key resource in managing the culture of innovation, rather than managing laboratories, scientists, and facilities that physically house innovation.

On a quarterly basis, the heroes of a company are those who generate the biggest profit margins. They are celebrated by Wall Street and proclaimed in news releases from the CEO. Every company must have a culture that places profitability in a key position and, the culture of a company must contain the seeds for its own future as well. Innovation, research, and process improvement are all conducted with the goal of profiting in the future. By the time the contribution is profitable, the research group or the CTO domain has long since handed it over to design and production. Their contribution can be quickly forgotten and all recognition given to the team that designed, produced, or sold the product.

The CTO office must insure that the company rewards, encourages, and places value in the actions of the research teams just as it does the production teams. Left untended or unappreciated, the energy of innovation will sputter and die. Innovation culture management must include credit for contributions to new products. It requires personnel processes that allow people to create in their own style—driven to be productive, but not driven to conform to a production lifestyle.

Once brought into existence, such an environment will attract people eager to be encouraged and facilitated in their work rather than controlled, ignored, and marginalized. Each of these people is an ingredient whose influence on the group and the culture must be managed to prevent corruption of the culture, but not to prevent its productive evolution or to enforce conformity.

Innovate

The most valuable innovation that the CTO office can contribute to a corporation is in creating and leading a process for improvement. Scientists in laboratories are the innovators of new products, components, and processes, but structuring the company's approach to managing, commercializing, and improving the innovation process is an essential task. Henry Chesbrough explored the different business models for innovation that have been used at Xerox Palo Alto Research Center (PARC), IBM T.J. Watson Research Center, Intel Corporation, and Lucent. Though all contained brilliant scientists who were making significant strides in new technologies, each practiced a different business model for commercializing their inventions (Chesbrough, 2003).

The Xerox PARC model worked very well for a company that dominated the market for photocopiers, but, was not adept at creating and entering new business areas—such as personal computers, networking, and peripherals. The stories of Xerox's failures in the latter area are well documented (Smith & Alexander, 1999).

IBM, Intel, and Lucent have all taken these lessons to heart and practice a very different model than their predecessors at PARC. IBM has created a model for commercializing innovation that includes the traditional role of research at its roots. But they go much further than that. They have explored the role of a system integrator of industry standard components—the IBM personal computer. They also license new technologies to competitors. In one case, they created a 2½" hard drive for their own laptop computers. In addition to using it to improve the sales of the IBM ThinkPad, they also licensed the drives to other vendors and doubled the revenues generated from the hard drive technology. IBM has gone on to license pure intellectual property before it has become a product at all.

The innovation business model as practiced by IBM is one of the key contributions that can come from the CTO office. Chesbrough explains the importance of the Open Innovation business model (Chesbrough, 2003). He has documented the transformation of innovation processes from a closed corporate lab to an open collaboration among companies that can mutually benefit from working together.

Hargadon also explored the evolution of the innovation process (Hargadon, 2003), but his work focused on a different aspect. Specifically, he exploded the myth of the lone inventor creating new technologies from an individual, personal effort and inspiration. From Thomas Edison to the modern academic researcher, Hargadon reveals that these mythic heroes are really at the center of multiple networks of knowledge. They borrow ideas from one field and apply them in another. They also benefit from the hard work of a team of people that are largely unheralded in later accounts. Businesses have discovered that inventions sell better when they come from a single, inspiring inventor. So, they have used the press to create images that are much more heroic than was really the case.

Understanding this type of mythology is an important role within a company. Strategists and planners must pursue innovation models based on successful practice rather than on the mythology of the individual hero.

Implement

Business models, strategic plans, and visions are fantastic starting points, but they exist for the sole purpose of implementation—to change behavior within an organization. The CTO must follow-up on all of these and track their implementation. If they remain concepts on paper, then the organization will be robbed of their power. Rewards and punishments must be tied to the successful implementation of innovation models. Progress needs to be measured in order to determine when rewards should be bestowed.

The CTO office must implement a process for encouraging the use of business models for innovation. In organizations like Intel Corp., the innovators fall under the organizational control of the CTO. In this case, overseeing and motivating changes is within the sphere of control of the CTO. However, in other organizations, the innovators may be assigned to specific business units of geographic offices. Under this structure, the CTO office must build relationships with these dispersed offices and create partnerships in improving innovation using many of the tools described in previous sections.

Conclusion

The position and responsibilities of the Chief Technology Officer and his or her support organization have been evolving for a relatively short period of time. The title has been used for approximately 20 years—evolving first from the Director of Research and later emerging as the technical partner in a technology start-up. It has been applied as a near-synonym for the CIO in an IT services organization, and as a technology executive contributing strategic decisions in multinational companies. With such a wide variety of implementation, it is not surprising that the position has been poorly defined.

The spectrum presented in this paper illustrates many of the recurrent responsibilities of the CTO and the CTO office. The position, under a variety of names, has become more essential to businesses each year. The technology component of products and services and the rapid pace of innovation combine to create a competitive environment in which technology and innovation are essential ingredients for success. Past centuries have witnessed predominance of production, finance, government relationships—and now technology. The CTO office has critical responsibilities to the organization and the importance of these will continue to increase throughout this century.

4

STRATEGIC RESPONSIBILITIES
AND RELATIONSHIPS

The significant role of technology in strategic business decisions has created the need for executives who understand technology and recognize profitable applications to products, services, and processes. Many companies have addressed this need through the appointment of a Chief Technology Officer (CTO) whose responsibilities include monitoring new technologies and assessing their potential to become new products or services, overseeing the selection of research projects to insure that they have the potential to add value to the company, providing reliable technical assessments of potential mergers and acquisitions, explaining company products and future plans to the trade media, and participating in government, academic, and industry groups where there are opportunities to promote the company's reputation and to capture valuable data.

Integrating these technology-based activities into the corporate strategy requires that the CTO nurture effective relationships with key people throughout the company. These include the CEO, members of the Executive Committee, chief scientists, research laboratory directors, and marketing leaders.

Origins of the Chief Technology Officer

In the 1950s and 1960s, many large corporations established beautiful research laboratories at locations remote from their headquarters and manufacturing facilities. The goal was to collect brilliant scientists and allow them to study relevant topics in an environment unhindered by day-to-day business concerns. The director of the laboratory was often a corporate vice president who did not participate in decisions regarding corporate strategy and direction. Instead, his responsibilities were to attract the best scientists, explore new ideas, and publish respected research papers (Larson, 2001).

By the late 1980s, companies began to anoint R&D laboratory directors as Chief Technology Officers. Technology was becoming such a prevalent part of company products and services that senior management needed an operational executive who could understand it and provide reliable advice on its application. However, executive search agencies, under direction from their corporate customers, continued to fill the CTO position with the same people they had recommended leading R&D laboratories (Parker, 2002). Several experiences with these candidates soon made it clear that the responsibilities of the CTO were significantly different from those of the research scientist. The CTO position called for a technologist or scientist who could translate technological capabilities into strategic business decisions. Lewis expresses this very clearly.

> *"The CTO's key tasks are not those of lab director writ large but, rather, of a technical businessperson deeply involved in shaping and implementing overall corporate strategy."* (Lewis and Lawrence, 1990)

Though large companies such as General Electric, Allied-Signal, and ALCOA created the position of CTO in the late 1980s, the position has also played an important role in computer and Internet companies in the late 1990s. Many of these provide products and services that are pure technology. Therefore, the CTO can play a prominent role in directing and shaping their entire business.

Strategic Responsibilities of the CTO

The CTO position is far from being standardized. Each company has unique requirements for its CTO and provides a unique organizational structure into which the person will fit. This section describes some of the more prominently cited responsibilities of the CTO.

Monitoring and Assessing New Technologies

The rate of change of technology guarantees that knowledge and expertise gained several years ago will no longer be completely valid. This creates the need for a technologically current person to serve as an advisor to senior executives during strategic decision-making. Paul O'Neill stated that a CTO should be expected to, *"identify, access, [and] investigate high-risk, high-return technologies possessing potential application within existing businesses or for creating new businesses"* (O'Neill and Bridenbaugh, 1992). Knowledge that is several years old cannot effectively guide this type of assessment. If a company is planning to modify its production process or add new products, it must understand how the latest technologies can contribute to those plans. As an illustration of this, Peter Bridenbaugh recognized the significance of technical advancements that made it possible for mini-mills to operate profitably and to assault the markets held by large metal producing companies like Alcoa. Because he was actively monitoring new technologies and assessing their applicability to business opportunities, Bridenbaugh was in a position to advise Alcoa of this threat while mini-mills still occupied a very limited niche in metals production. Though other executives within Alcoa had come up through the operational and scientific ranks, their focus had changed to organizational and financial issues. Because they were no longer intimately familiar with the latest scientific developments in metal production, the emergence of mini-mills did not appear to be a serious threat to Alcoa's business. Junior engineers, on the other hand, may have realized that new technology made it possible for small mills to produce high quality products at prices competitive to Alcoa's. But, those engineers did not possess the experience necessary to support their opinions to upper management. Neither did they have access to those senior decision-makers. Therefore, a CTO who embodies current knowledge, is networked with company engineers, has years of experience, and has access to executive decision-makers is a valuable resource in recognizing important new technologies and bringing them into the company's strategic decision-making process.

Bert Thurlings of Philips Research Laboratories has arrived at conclusions similar to those of O'Neill and Bridenbaugh through his field studies of numerous CTOs. These indicate that CTOs themselves feel that one of their most important responsibilities is to monitor, evaluate, and select technologies that can be applied to future products and services (Thurlings and Debackere, 1996). A significant investment in the active exploration of all relevant technical areas is required in order to identify opportunities buried amid all of the information available. Internal company managers and scientists are often qualified to perform this analysis, but are so focused on day-to-day operations that they do not have time to study broadly and deeply enough to locate the technologies that will be essential in the future. These people frequently identify important changes once a competitor has already implemented a similar idea. However, by that time, it is too late for the company to capture the lead in the application of that technology to products, services, and production techniques. Such a company would find itself trying to catch-up to the new leader in the field.

The opinions and experiences expressed by large companies like Alcoa and Philips are echoed by the CTOs of the new generation of information companies as well. Pavan Nigam, CTO of WebMD, reports that an important part of his job is reading and evaluating large amounts of data about new products (Aspatore, 2000). Information service vendors are so eager to attract the attention of the media and of customers that their claims are often exaggerated. Managers and scientists within WebMD could be misled by these claims and expend irreplaceable time and money working with products that are not able to deliver the promised capabilities. Therefore, Nigam provides a valuable service by remaining abreast of vendor claims and by learning about the experiences of other companies using those same products and services. This allows him to direct WebMD away from ineffective products and toward others that do solve its problems.

Darren McKnight, the CTO of defense contractor Titan Corp., listed the evaluation of new technologies as his number one responsibility (2002). After Titan developed an electron beam technology to sterilize medical components and the company's senior technologists recognized that this capability could also be used to pasteurize food products—Titan created the Surebeam subsidiary to pursue this market. Following the anthrax contaminations in Washington, D.C., McKnight and others recognized that Surebeam's systems could be used to kill anthrax hidden in postal envelopes. Backed by existing research and prior publications on the subject, Titan created a new market for electron beam systems and assigned a facility to sterilize selected mail destined for the nation's capital. The expertise of business executives, unaided by technologists, would not have been sufficient for identifying such a unique opportunity. Situations like this demonstrate the real contributions that can be made by a CTO.

Strategic Innovation

Michael Porter explains that, *"companies have to find ways of grow-ing and building advantages rather than just eliminating disadvantages"* (Gibson, 1998). A significant part of this is strategic innovation. In some industries, new products based on new technology are the lifeblood of the company. In other industries, core products remain unchanged for decades, but the processes used to create them are continually evolv-ing and becoming more efficient. Proctor & Gamble recognized that their products were mature, but that their scientists had a number of good ideas for improving existing products and creating new ones. The company's CEO and CTO created the Innovation Leadership Team to find and allocate funds to support these new ideas. This pro-gram quickly led to eleven new products and a number of innovations waiting to be turned into products, giving Proctor & Gamble a signifi-cant lead on competitors (Brunner, 2001). Just as Peter Bridenbaugh learned that emerging technology was creating a new class of com-petitors for rolled metal products, companies that create commodities like laundry detergent, toilet paper, gasoline, and furniture must apply technology to improve their production processes and add an edge to their products that competitors cannot match. O'Neill emphasizes that established companies need a CTO to *"assure development of funda-mental technologies offering clear competitive advantage for current and future businesses."* Walter Robb, former CTO of General Electric Medi-cal Systems, believes that *"it is the responsibility of the CTO to push the boundary on risk taking"* (Robb, 1994). The CTO's relationships with the R&D scientists equip him with knowledge about the state-of-the-art that will allow him to recommend risks that have a high probability of success. GE's innovative designs for CAT scanners and magnetic resonance imaging systems accepted high levels of risk in order to create unique products containing features beyond the technical reach of their competitors. Those calculated risks led to a market dominating position that extended over a decade.

CTOs like Robb take risks because they have a vision for where the company should take its products in the future. Such product vision is one of the key reasons for employing a CTO. Ron Moritz, CTO of Symantec, says:

> *"One of the key roles of the CTO is to provide the technical vision to complement the business vision, setting the tone and direction for the company's technologies. Leadership, in this context, comes from being able to set the technical course and from being able to define what the company's products and technologies might look like in two, three, or more years."* (Aspatore, 2000)

Product vision should be based on an intimate understanding of the power of the current technology component of the product and knowledge about innovations and changes that are occurring in related fields.

Michael Earl emphasized that investments in technology and innovation must be connected directly to business strategy. In fact, he found that the most successful approach was when a company did not have a separate technology strategy. Instead, the best technology strategies were those that were fully integrated with the business strategy (Earl and Feeny, 1994). CTOs are now expected to contribute technology expertise to business strategies, not to create independent research laboratories and strategies that are only loosely coupled to the company's profit engine.

Mergers and Acquisitions

Mergers and acquisitions (M&A) are an important part of the growth strategy of many companies. These involve important strategies in financing, governmental oversight, taxation, corporate culture, and technological synergy. Unfortunately, after studying more than 5,000 acquisitions, divestitures, spin-offs, equity investments, and alliances, Frick and Torres discovered that over half of the deals resulted in a lower market value for the resulting entities (Frick and Torres, 2002). Other McKinsey studies in the late 1980's reported that, at that time, more than seventy percent of acquisitions failed to earn back the cost of capital used to purchase the company (Parker, 2002). Frick and Torres maintain that there are two major causes of this problem. First, the acquisition becomes an exercise in financial engineering. It focuses on successfully structuring the finances required to make the acquisition possible and loses sight of the strategic objectives of the acquisition. Second, it is a form of corporate ego boosting. Corporate leaders are eager to build an empire or capture high profile products. Frick and Torres contend that, in contrast to these two motives, value creating mergers and acquisitions are focused on the strategic value that can be achieved through the transaction. However, to make this happen, it is essential that the due diligence leading up to the deal include an evaluation of the value of the technologies being acquired. The CTO's role in due diligence includes evaluating patents, reviewing technical publications, and studying trade data to determine the value of the target company and to rank it against its competitors. Darren McKnight at Titan Corporation includes these types of investigations in his list of key responsibilities. At Titan each deal has included a strategic evaluation of the technologies within the target company and the synergies that those technologies could generate within the Titan family.

Marketing and Media Relations

Media attention to company products and capabilities plays an important role in the success of those products. Constructing the information and images released to the public is primarily the responsibility of the marketing and sales departments. However, technical expertise is required to accurately translate some product details into terms that can be marketed. Rajeev Bharadwaj, the CTO of Ejasent, plays an active role in communicating with the media (2002). He believes that the CTO must translate technical details into real customer advantages that are superior to those of competing products. Internet start-ups must also create convincing presentations and demonstrations for venture capitalists (VCs). The VCs provide the initial revenue stream necessary to turn an idea into a viable product. In the early stages of a company, the VCs are the customers and the marketing story is focused on them rather than the actual consumers.

In addition to creating media worthy stories for publication, companies create media worthy experts to be interviewed and quoted. Trade magazines and television producers rely upon statements by insiders and experts who can speak authoritatively on a subject. These experts *"are like politicians—they're made, nurtured, and coached"* (Gibson, 1998). They are also made constantly accessible to the media for consultation. Ron Moritz, CTO of Symantec, was an expert in Internet security, but the media was not aware of his expertise. Therefore, Symantec's President took it upon himself to turn Moritz into a media recognized and consulted expert. This was part of the corporate strategy at Symantec and contributed to the success of its security products.

Government, Academia, Professional Organizations

Prominent technologists are often called upon to provide services to government, academic, and professional organizations. These services combine civic and professional duty with the opportunity to convey a positive image of the company and its products.

Governmental committees investigate issues of national importance. Service on these committees is an honor, but it also requires the dedication of time, energy, and money that could be focused on other pursuits. Participation brings several rewards that are an alternative form of payment.

* Tacit recognition as a leader in the field,
* Opportunities to influence the decisions of the committee in a professionally positive manner, and
* Early and intimate access to the work generated by the committee.

Since many CTOs possess advanced college degrees, they tend to have multiple relationships with members of academia. These relationships lead to partnerships and funding for research that is of mutual interest. Companies participating in these activities generally structure the partnership such that they have first access to the results of the research. One of the most commercially successful and widely recognized industry/academia partnerships is the Media Lab at MIT. This lab investigates the application of computer technologies to practical social problems. In 2001, the lab received 95% of its $36 million budget from 140 corporate sponsors. There are hundreds of similar, but smaller, examples of corporate and academic partnerships that can involve participation or oversight by the CTO. As a businessman, the CTO must insure that money and time spent on such projects is aligned with the corporate strategy and has a realistic potential of contributing to the company's competitive advantage in the foreseeable future.

Finally, CTOs are called upon to participate in professional organizations and their associated meetings. Similar to government committees, these are an opportunity to project a positive image within the profession and to communicate important messages. Presentations allow the CTO to tell partners, suppliers, competitors, and customers about their expertise, products, future strategy, or commitment to an industry. Both, Bill Waite, President of Aegis Technologies, and David Zeltzer, CTO of the Fraunhofer Center for Research in Computer Graphics, maintain that the relationships that they build through professional organizations contribute directly to their business base.

Company Culture

Earlier sections described how the CTO could contribute to strategy, acquisitions, media relations, government committees, and academic research. But, the CTO can also serve an important role in creating the internal culture. The CTO should initiate activities and policies that create a technology-friendly culture aligned with the company's business strategy.

Other technology leaders throughout a company may create policies and practices that attempt to attract and retain the highest quality people available. However, if these are not aligned with the corporate business strategy, they may attract excellent people who are not able to contribute to business objectives.

The CTO should insure that policies and practices are constructed to attract the right kind, right number, and right placement of technologists. This will require the establishment of formal and informal networks to implement the policies and to insure that they are aligned throughout the company (Lewis and Lawrence, 1990). These networks will also serve as the conduits through which corporate vision and direction can be communicated.

Informal networks of technologists can be used to mediate organizational problems that extend beyond the control of operational managers. In some companies these networks tend to catalyze unofficial practices that are aimed at improving internal performance. Lewis reports the emergence of internal publications, technical seminars, lists of known experts, and technical expositions.

Skills and Competencies of an Effective CTO

Companies increasingly need strong technical people who want to master business strategy and apply their expertise toward the future growth prospects of the company.

Technology. The CTO should have been a leader in a technology that is an important part of the corporate business base. No CTO can master all of the technologies used by a diverse company— for that the CTO will rely on an internal technology network.

Strategy. The CTO is a corporate executive dealing with strategic decisions about the future direction of the company. The CTO must make the transition from technical expert to business strategists and be prepared to spend significant time and energy on business issues that are tangential to the company's technology (e.g. mergers and acquisitions, government regulations, intellectual property rights).

Business Growth. Chief Scientists are in a position to pursue interesting technologies, but CTOs must make decisions about which technologies are most likely to generate the highest rate of return. The CTO thinks about technology as a moneymaking asset, not as a field of exploration for its own sake.

Interpersonal Skills. All executives, including the CTO, must be able to communicate clearly and effectively with people from all types of backgrounds (e.g. research, manufacturing, sales, accounting). Executives spend a significant amount of time retelling their vision for the company to insure that everyone is headed in the same direction.

Executive Relationships. The CTO position is relatively new in most organizations. Though the title appears to associate the person with the CEO, CFO, COO, and CIO, the individual filling the position must insure that he or she is included in executive meetings and decision-making. Early CIOs were viewed as "techies" rather than business strategists and had to demonstrate their value in contributing to corporate strategy. CTOs will face the same challenge. Personal relationships with other executives are an important part of making that happen.

Relationships that Empower the CTO

The CTO position was initially created to insure that senior management paid appropriate attention to their own corporate technological capability (Betz, 1993). Attracting this attention and operating as an effective member of the executive team, requires that the CTO nurture relationships with a number of people and groups internal and external to the company.

Chief Executive Officer and Executive Committees

Providing strategic advice to the CEO and the Executive Committee requires much more than technical expertise. The CTO must earn the trust and confidence of the CEO. In previous positions, the CTO may have earned the respect and confidence of peers and superiors through technical prowess and performance. But, this new position requires business prowess and financial performance. The CTO must exhibit a clear understanding of and dedication to improving the competitive position of the company.

The acceptance of the CTO as a business strategist is an important step. It will determine whether the CTO is treated as an equal member of the executive team or is isolated as an outside source for technical advice and information. Ed Roberts' study of the strategic management of technology indicates that most companies include the CTO on the Executive Committee along with the CEO, COO, CFO, and CIO. In North America 60% of the companies surveyed included the CTO on this committee. In Europe the number was 67% and in Japan it was 91% (Gwynne, 1996). In some companies the CTO actually teaches senior management about the importance of technology in their industry. The goal is to ingrain technology as a significant consideration in all executive decision-making (Gwynne, 1996; Earl and Feeny, 2000).

CTOs are not the first officers to face the challenge of inclusion or exclusion from the strategic process. When the CIO position emerged, they too were branded as technologists who could not function as business strategists (Kwak, 2001). This image has diminished as CIOs have shown themselves to be just as effective at making business decisions as their management-schooled peers. Kwak cites the results of a study of pairs of executives at 69 companies that indicated that the business acumen of CIOs was equal to that of their executive peers. Another study of 417 construction company executives found that eighty percent of the CIOs in those companies were considered equal contributors of the strategic decision making process (Phair and Rubin, 1998). Therefore, the CTO should be able to learn from the integration experience of the CIO. Executive Committee members should also recognize that the technological stereotype that was not accurate for the CIO might also prove to be inaccurate for the CTO.

If the CTO is to provide business decisions and advice, there needs to be some measure of the quality of this advice. The CTOs performance should be measured against a plan worked out with the CEO. This plan may include achieving milestones, introducing new products, reducing costs, reducing uncertainty, and selecting the right research projects to fund. Bill Waite advocates a customized set of metrics for the CTO. Within his company, these included maintaining and teaching technology within the organization, measuring the speed at which technology is brought into the organization, the rate at which the CTO turns technology into salable intellectual property, and the CTO's effectiveness as the custodian for research and development money.

Chief Information Officer

Many organizations have a difficult time separating the responsibilities of the CTO from those of the CIO, which can make the working relationship between the two very difficult. At the 2001 InfoWorld CTO Forum, CTOs from Sun Microsystems, eBay, Dell Computer, and other companies identified their responsibilities as being externally focused while the CIO's responsibilities were internally focused (Spiers, 2001). Corporations have realized that they need a CIO to oversee the application of technology to internal operations. This has included computer systems for accounting, billing, telephony, security, and a host of other functions. Prior to the creation of the CTO position, the CIO was the only executive technologist and was often called upon to support manufacturing computerization, the purchase of computer aided design packages, and strategic decisions for injecting technology into products (Kwak, 2001).

The internal/external division of responsibilities is a very useful differentiation, but it leaves significant gray areas that can result in turf wars between the two players. Therefore, the CTO's relationship with the CIO should be based on a more clearly defined division of responsibility. The goal is to create a complementary and supportive relationship that maximizes contributions to corporate strategy and profitability.

Chief Scientists

Chief Scientists are much more intimately involved in the day-to-day execution of scientific and technical projects. Each of these is usually limited to the laboratory, division, or facility in which he or she resides. As described earlier, senior technologists are often very eager to explore new areas. But, these explorations should be harnessed to contribute to the company's strategic direction. Earl maintained that a company should not have a separate technology strategy. Supporting this perspective, one study has found that short-term, product focused R&D is positively correlated with the financial performance of the company, while long-term R&D is negatively correlated with it. That is one reason that it is important for the CTO to mentor the Chief Scientists and to direct their focus such that it contributes to the success of the company.

Chief Scientists may also have informal networks of technologists that span business areas, but they do not have the official charter to cross-pollinate technologies. The CTO can organize an internal council of technologists to search out and apply the best technologies available across the company. Darren McKnight of Titan reports that he sponsored internal summits to bring leading technologists together to share ideas. He viewed it as his responsibility to create leverage across many different business groups to identify potential combinations of technology that could become new products or services. He is currently working on plans to create a network of technologists similar to that described by Brunner.

CMGI was one of the leading incubators of the Internet business explosion. Daniel Jaye, the CTO of Engage, a CMGI incubated company, felt that the cross-pollination of technologies within CMGI could identify valuable opportunities and solve local problems. Therefore, acting as the ad hoc CTO of the parent company, he organized technology summits for all CMGI technology leaders. One of these summits led to the realization that two CMGI companies were buying services from the same vendor. The leaders reasoned that the vendor would be a good fit under the CMGI umbrella and purchased the company, reducing outsourcing costs and adding a proven product to the CMGI family.[6]

Research and Development Laboratories

Since the 1960s, research and development laboratories have been transformed from independent scientists working on challenging, but questionably marketable technologies, to organizations that are expected to make direct contributions to company profits. The CTO can play an important role in monitoring and directing these labs. Erickson recommends several principles that a CTO should use for directing R&D. First R&D personnel should be kept in touch with the company's customers and markets (Erickson et al, 1990). Few labs can seclude themselves from the market and conduct research for its own sake. Second, the CTO should foster open communications between R&D staff, manufacturing engineers, and the marketing department. Third, the CTO should hold the R&D labs to schedule and budget commitments. If an R&D project is not delivering results, it may need to be terminated and the funds applied more productively elsewhere. Some long-standing projects constantly show great promise and absorb resources, but produce nothing. These projects, though considered "pillars of the lab," must be held accountable and face termination if they do not produce results.

R&D laboratory budgets should be the topic of critical reviews by the executive staff. The CTO should lead initial funding reviews in which R&D projects present the expectations for the project, its applicability to market needs, the position relative to competitors, and a record of past successes. The CTO should also hold in-progress reviews to monitor problems and successes. A CTO can serve as an honest broker in these reviews because he or she comes from outside of the laboratory and is not personally involved in the projects.

Sales and Marketing

CTOs like Rajeev Bharadwaj at Ejasent and Ron Moritz at Symantec are actively involved in marketing products and services. These CTOs recognize that some products are so technically sophisticated that explaining them to the trade media requires a technical representative. When the CTO is used to explain the subtle, but significant, differences between the company's products and those of competitors, he or she becomes a de facto member of the marketing staff (Foster, 2000).

Working with the sales and marketing departments also insures that the CTO remains rooted in the customers' need for the product, rather than the technical sophistication of the product. Supporting this perspective, Michael Wolfe of Kana Communications says that, *"Creating a product is mapping what a customer needs to what you can build"* (Aspatore, 2000). Making this mapping requires regular and detailed interactions with customers and the marketplace.

Technology and Executive Leadership

Companies began adding Chief Technology Officers to the executive ranks in the 1980s because technology was becoming an integral part of many strategic decisions and future plans. The CIO already provided strong expertise on the internal application of technology. But, senior managers needed expert advice regarding the inclusion of technologies in existing products and the creation of new products and services with large technical components. A CTO that is actively involved in monitoring new technologies, separating marketing rhetoric from technical facts, and identifying profitable applications for those technologies can make a significant difference in the company's competitive future. The CTO can also add value to the company by participating in government, academic, and industry groups in a manner that creates positive attention for the company.

Technology companies are involved in thousands of acquisitions every year. Selecting the best target for an acquisition often requires reliable advice on technical issues at the executive level. The CTO is also a valuable tool in addressing the increasingly well-informed media about the products, services, and the future plans of the company. CTOs can speak as peers to other technologists and can play a role in convincing the media that the company's decisions are sound and will add value for the company's stakeholders.

It is important that the CTO not become the senior technologist of the company. Instead, he or she is the senior business executive with a focus on technology. In the CTO position, senior management is not looking for enthusiastic advice from a research scientist. Instead, they need sound advice on business decisions involving technology.

Position	Comparing Roles and Responsibilities
CTO	*Technology Strategy.* The CTO's primary responsibility is contributing to the strategic direction of the company by identifying the role that specific technologies will play in its future growth. The CTO looks for contributions that technology can make to the competitive advantage of the company.
	Internal Coordination. Identification of the best technologies usually comes from a strong internal network of people who are in touch with the latest technologies and understand their potential.
	External Partnerships. Like all business professionals, the CTO will be part of a strong network that includes business partners, academics, government officials, and technology thought leaders.
CIO	*Information Technology Application.* The CIO leads the application of information technology to internal processes and services. This person is responsible for improving the efficiency of internal systems like payroll, accounting, accounts receivable, labor recording, benefits management, human resources records, government reporting, and a number of others.
	Reduce Internal Operating Costs. The CIO's systems are focused on reducing the costs associated with the company operations listed above.
	Improve Services to Employees and Partners. CIOs and IT departments have provided fantastic improvements in employee services in the last two decades. They have also built systems that allow better information and financial exchange with business partners.
Chief Scientist	*Technology Creation.* Chief Scientists lead teams that are focused on creating new technologies. Given strategic direction from management, these teams work to create products or services that make the company's strategy possible and that do so in a manner superior to their competitors.
	Recognized Leader. Chief Scientists should be recognized leaders in their technical field. They should be actively involved in professional associations and conferences with their peers in industry and academia.

5

STRATEGIC ALIGNMENT OF TECHNOLOGICAL COMPETENCIES, CAPABILITIES, AND RESOURCES

Prahalad and Hamel introduced core competencies in 1990 and started a stream of thought and discussion on the subject. Along the way, the importance of identifying and fostering corporate "capabilities" has been confused with creating competencies. In this paper, we differentiate these two terms and show that each refers to a different set of essential practices within the organization. Competencies refer to unique products or services, often created in the R&D labs, which can penetrate existing markets. Capabilities are the operational ability to deliver those new products and services efficiently, repeatedly, and in sufficient volume. Capabilities and competencies are both required to successfully place a product in the market. These must also be supported by corporate resources to insure longevity. The importance of aligning competencies, capabilities, and resources is explained through the analogy of an axe blade penetrating dense lumber.

Competencies

"Core Competencies are the collective learning in the organization, especially how to coordinate diverse production skills and integrate multiple streams of technologies" (Prahalad & Hamel, 1990). The introduction of core competencies had a major impact on management practice and thinking. Multiple authors adopted, adapted, and extended the ideas of core competencies. One of the most prevalent adaptations was to change "competency" to "capability" and apply a more general definition to the term. Stalk, et al, stated that, *"whereas core competence emphasizes technological and production expertise at specific points along the value chain, capabilities are more broadly based; encompassing the entire value chain"* (Stalk, Evans, & Shulman, 1992). They go on to propose that core capability is *"a set of business processes strategically understood"*

and that it represents *"technological and production expertise at specific points along the value chain."* Leonard-Barton turned core competency into core capability in this way; *"core capability is an interrelated, interdependent knowledge system"* (Leonard-Barton, 1992). Teece, Pisano, and Shuen modified the idea and named it "dynamic capabilities" to emphasize the active and continuously changing nature of maintaining organizational capabilities. They recognized that "static capabilities" were severely limited and that really valuable "capabilities" required constantly adapting to new situations (Teece, Pisano, & Shuen, 2001). Even Hamel and Prahalad sometimes use the terms interchangeably in their later writings (Hamel & Prahalad, 1994). These adaptations have contributed to the widespread confusion of the meaning of the two terms.

In this paper, I propose that there is an important distinction to be made between competency and capability. Providing different definitions of these two terms is valuable in aligning two different sets of practices within a company. This alignment is essential to the effective penetration of the market with new and existing products. I propose that capabilities refer to a broad set of practices in which a company has proficiency, but that these practices are rooted in daily operations. A capability is the organizational ability to execute activities repetitively, efficiently, and predictably.

In contrast, a competency refers to a company's ability to improve its performance continuously. "Improved performance" may refer to better production efficiency, financial ratios, marketing effectiveness, or product development. A competency is the source of differentiation for the company allowing it to create and offer unique products, services, and solutions to customers. A competency is the organizational ability to improve continuously.

Furthermore, established companies possess many more capabilities than they do competencies. They have developed the ability to execute repetitively in a number of areas. However, they have relatively few competencies, or areas in which they are able to improve their performance continuously. In contrast, new companies have relatively more competencies and fewer capabilities. Their entire business strategy is based on a few things that they can do differently than established industry leaders, but they possess very few capabilities to deliver products and services consistently and efficiently.

Market Penetration

In order to penetrate the market, a company must be able to align both its capabilities and its competencies for effective satisfaction of customer needs. Established markets are filled with products that meet the needs of a specific set of customers. New entrants into the market must provide either a better product or a different product in order to displace those that already exist. Porter emphasized two sustainable strategies of entering and remaining in an industry. A company must be able to offer the same products at a lower cost, or they must be able to offer differentiated products that cannot easily be duplicated by competitors (Porter, 1985). Christensen extended this perspective by demonstrating the power of technological advancements to enable a low-cost strategy to be transformed into a differentiated product (Christensen, 1999). Christensen's disruptive innovation brings out the power of technology to create major competitors from companies that previously would have been permanently relegated to the role of a niche player.

Given the opportunities presented by low cost, differentiated products, and technology disruption, a company must structure itself to deliver these advantages consistently, repetitively, and efficiently to customers. Without a complementary strategy across the company, a new product or service cannot be pressed forward to create a permanent and growing position in the market.

In addition to competencies and capabilities, a company must align its resources to feed the production and management systems that deliver the volume and quality of products needed. Essential resources include personnel, technology, information, finances, and natural resources.

Strategic Alignment: The Axe Analogy

Companies have competencies, capabilities, and resources. All of these must be aligned to be effective in penetrating the market. Without such alignment, a product or service might have sufficient financial resources, but insufficient production capability. It may have world-class manufacturing capabilities, but poor R&D and innovation competencies to create new products. Applying resources, capabilities, and competencies individually or without alignment is not an effective strategy for market penetration. Fuchs et al strongly emphasized that the alignment or integration of these three factors is as important as managing any one of them individually. They suggest that many companies fail, not because they have poor capabilities, competencies, or resources, but because they do a very poor job of aligning them toward their strategic objectives (Fuchs, et al, 2000).

This idea is illustrated with the analogy of an axe splitting wood (Figure 5.1). The wood represents the market that is to be penetrated. It is dense with existing products and services. There are also inter-locking relationships among products because a customer uses many of these together. In order to enter this market, a new product must provide a better solution and it must be able to break existing bonds.

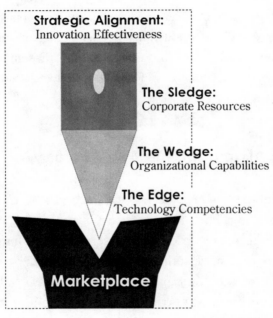

Figure 5.1 An axe penetrating wood is an apt analogy of the power of strategically aligning competencies, capabilities, and resources to achieve and maintain significant market penetration.

The sharp edge of the axe blade represents the core competencies of the company to improve its performance such as through creating better products or better production methods. The edge is honed through research and development, the application of new materials, the creation of new state-of-the-art production capabilities, or the application of products from an adjacent industry. This sharp edge penetrates the market and separates established relationships between products, services, and customers.

Separating established relationships is not sufficient for taking market share. Following the edge, there must be an organizational wedge that is designed to push aside competing products and replace them with the new competitor's products. The wedge represents the capabilities of the company to continuously deliver the products and services. This includes manufacturing, logistics, marketing, partnerships, labor relations, and a host of other capabilities to follow-up on the disruptive entry of the edge of the axe into the market.

Finally, there is the sledge. This represents the resources of the company to continue to feed competencies and capabilities. The resource sledge includes the people, factories, logistics systems, natural resources, and finances necessary to push the edge and wedge deeper into the market; opening a wider space for the new competitor's products and services.

Using this analogy, we can also demonstrate the limitations associated with applying any one of these individually. Resources alone deliver a blunt object against established products and relationships. It is like chopping wood with a sledge hammer; it may dent the surface and disrupt some small part of the market, but it will not penetrate (Figure 5.2a). Large oil, gas, and gold producing companies are heavy users of resources that could attempt to enter a new market applying purely the brute force of their resources.

Competencies alone can penetrate the surface and break some relationships, but without capabilities, this will make only a small cut into the marketplace. There is no wedge behind the edge to open a significant space for the new products or services (Figure 5.2b). Many R&D focused start-up companies are based entirely on competencies. They have excellent skills in a narrow area, but lack the ability to apply them effectively; such as through effective marketing, distribution, customer service, or information processing.

Capabilities alone do not possess the edge to break into the market or the resource sledge to deliver significant force behind the blow (Figure 5.2c). A large, low-cost manufacturing company typically has significant capabilities, but without either unique competencies or abundant resources. It is important to have all three aligned to effectively penetrate the market.

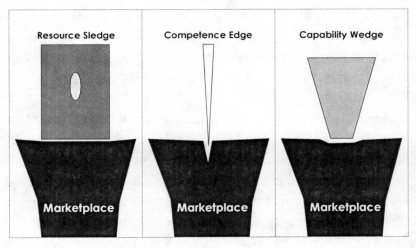

Figure 5.2 Individually neither resources, competency, nor capability are effective at market penetration.

Competencies: The Edge

In their 1990 HBR paper, Prahalad and Hamel state that, *"core competencies are the collective learning in the organization, especially how to coordinate diverse production skills and integrate multiple streams of technologies."* They go on to emphasize that core competence should: (1) provide potential access to a wide variety of markets, (2) make a significant contribution to the perceived customer benefits of the end product, and (3) be difficult for competitors to imitate [1]. In their 1994 book, *Competing for the Future*, these same authors provide a much more distinct definition that is more useful to us in differentiating competencies from capabilities. They state that, *"a core competence is a tapestry; woven from the threads of distinct skills and technologies. ... Many companies have had difficulty blending the multiple streams of science or technology that comprise their heritage into new, higher-order competencies"* (Hamel & Prahalad, 1994).

These new higher-order competencies refer to a company's ability to improve continuously. Investments in R&D are one traditional method of continuous improvement. To remain relevant and valuable, competencies must be renewed and changed. They must be able to make *"significant contributions to perceived customer benefits"*. If competencies are not renewed, then the customer will move away from the solutions offered yesterday toward better solutions offered by new competitors.

Sharif emphasizes that a company's competencies must include an ability to seek out solutions, to ask questions, and to experiment with new ideas. It cannot limit itself to better efficiency with existing products and processes (a capability). Competence is "solution seeking" and requires the synthesis of ideas from many domains and time periods. It looks beyond what is practical, feasible, profitable, and immediately approachable. This aligns well with Christensen's description of the emergence of a disruptive product from roots that at first appear to be inferior to current solutions. The key is that the new roots have much greater future potential than the old roots. Seeing this, appreciating it, and pursuing it requires the freedom to look beyond current capabilities (Sharif, 1995 & 1999).

Organizational learning is an important ingredient in maintaining a competency. The organization must be able to absorb and integrate multiple streams of knowledge (Sharif, 1999). They must be able to share this knowledge across the organization in such a way that it can move from where it is discovered, created, or appreciated, to where it can be effectively applied. In many companies, strong organizational boundaries have the effect of fracturing core competencies because they separate complimentary knowledge, prevent communication, and disincentivize collaboration (Leonard-Barton, 1992).

Inside the organization, there must be entrepreneurs who are able to pursue new and innovative paths. These people must "learn to forget" (Sharif, 1999) about established practices and seek out new solutions (Sharif, 1995). Over time, these groups must even learn to forget about established competences. When a competence no longer meets customers' needs or cannot be extended further, it does not provide competitive advantage. Continuing to adhere to these exhausted competences is a "competence trap" (Levitt & March, 1998) or a "core rigidity" (Leonard-Barton, 1992).

Capabilities: The Wedge

"Whereas core competence emphasizes technological and production expertise at specific points along the value chain, capabilities are more broadly based; encompassing the entire value chain." Capabilities are *"a set of business processes strategically understood ... the key is to connect them to real customer needs"* (Stalk, Evans, & Shulman, 1992).

Capabilities are those things that the company can do well repetitively. Production, logistics, daily human resource management, and partnerships—executing these day in and day out; handling the constant stream of issues that threaten to break these systems is an important capability for the company. Stalk points to the business processes that are established to insure that the system continues to work. He calls for strategic investments in the support infrastructure for these capabilities. Investments can only be strategic if the strategy aligns capabilities with competencies and resources as argued above. The goal is to outperform the competition in the speed of response to customer needs, the consistency of the product specifications, an understanding of where the market is going and what it wants from its suppliers, and maintaining an agility to adapt to market and world changes.

Given a specific set of resources, a company's capabilities allow it to apply those in an efficient manner. These enable continuous and uninterrupted operations. Improvements to existing processes, practices, and partnerships are part of these capabilities because they address incremental improvements to existing practices based on knowledge about those practices. They are an integrated part of operations, rather than being purposefully separated from operations. The competency to improve refers to the ability to see a product or process differently and to design the next generation that will replace it, not simply modify it.

"Core capability is an interrelated, interdependent knowledge system" [3]. These relationships limit progressive improvements to a rate and opportunity that can be accommodated within the entire current system, which differentiates them from competencies.

Resources: The Sledge

Sharif (1995 & 1999) suggests that there are four types of technology resources that are applied by a company that is innovating in its products and services (Figure 5.3). He describes these as:

* Technoware—object-embodied physical facilities
* Humanware—person-embodied human talents
* Inforware—record-embodied codified knowledge
* Orgaware—organization-embodied operational schemes

He also accepts that there are financial and natural resources available which are not necessarily related to technology.

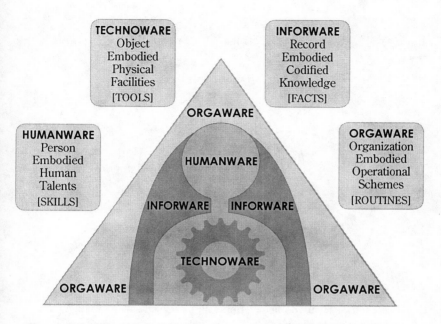

Figure 5.3 The technological resources available to a company fall into four major categories. *(Sharif, 1995)*

Leonard-Barton (1992) suggests that there are 4 dimensions (or resources) that make up the knowledge set that enables capabilities and competencies. These are:

* Skills and Knowledge Base—knowledge and skill embedded in employees (i.e. Humanware)
* Technical systems—knowledge embedded in technical systems (i.e. Technoware)
* Managerial systems—formal and informal ways of creating knowledge (i.e. Orgaware and Inforware)
* Values and Norms—traditions from the founders (i.e. Orgaware)

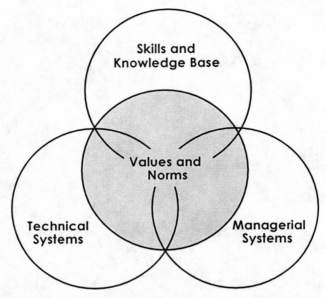

Figure 5.4 Leonard-Barton offers four dimensions of knowledge that contribute to organizational capabilities. *(Leonard-Barton, 1992)*

The resources categorized by both authors are those that make-up the sledge behind the blade of the axe. These resources put weight behind organizational capabilities and the technological competencies that are penetrating and opening a market. Resources enable the organization to function.

Alignment Strategy

"From a competitive strategy point of view, technology can be used defensively to sustain achieved advantage in product differentiation or cost, or offensively as an instrument to create new advantage in established lines of business or to develop new products and markets" (Burgelman, Christensen, & Wheelwright, 2004).

Burgelman also suggests that there are four dimensions of technology strategy:

* deployment of technology in the firm's product-market—position for differentiation (i.e. competencies),
* technology broadly applied across all activities of the firm's value chain (i.e. capabilities),
* resource commitment to various areas of technology (R&D) (i.e. resources), and
* use of organization design and management techniques to manage the technology function (i.e. daily operations).

These are consistent with the need to align competencies, capabilities, and resources in order to achieve significant and sustainable market penetration. In the introduction we also illustrated the effects of attacking the market with each one of these alone.

Attacking with resources alone refers to applying personnel, money, IP, or other assets without creating an organization that can deliver consistent products and services to companies. It also lacks the penetrating power of competencies to create new and innovative products that meet customer needs better than current offerings.

Attacking with competencies alone, creates a prototype product and attempts to enter the market without the production, logistic, and marketing efforts required to consistently deliver the product or to make customers aware of its existence.

Attacking with capabilities alone creates a production and delivery system for a product that is mediocre and lacking innovative solutions to customer problems. This may succeed in placing yet another product on the shelves, but it will not significantly impact the market. This approach is most effectively used when the differentiating feature of the product is merely its price.

Aligning all three of these creates an organization and a product that can make a unique place for itself in the market, maintain its momentum, and grow its market share over time. Apple Computers is a strong example of this type of alignment. Their competency is in creating unique products that are differentiated in style and power from PCs. That competency continuously adds new innovations to existing products (i.e. iMac) and creates entirely new products (i.e. iPod). They back this up with the capability to produce the products with high quality and insufficient quantities, accompanied by a marketing thrust that makes it clear why their offerings are unique and valuable. Behind these competencies and capabilities, are the resources in personnel (humanware), technology (technoware), and organizational structure (orgaware) to source new products. They also possess unique values and norms that give everyone in the organization permission to think, act, and create differently. Goggle is another company that appears to have aligned its competencies in Internet search and data analysis, with its capabilities to deliver targeted advertising based on search results, and supports these with abundant human and financial resources. The company continues to create new products like Google Maps, Earth, Desktop, Toolbar, Blogger, and Picassa; all of which build upon and extend their core competencies in collecting, analyzing, understanding, and selling data.

Conclusion

Prahalad and Hamel suggested that a company has only a few core competencies, and emphasized the fact that corporate strategy must be built around these competencies. In this paper we build on those authors' ideas to create a framework of competencies, capabilities, and resources which must work together to effectively penetrate a market. This alignment is an essential part of the company's technology innovation strategy. If these three pieces are not aligned, then a competency-based strategy will be ineffective because it will not be backed by the organizational processes or capabilities that are necessary to repeatedly carry those competencies to customers. Also, without sufficient resources, competencies and capabilities will be starved and unable to meet the demands of a market that has been penetrated. Initial successes will not persist long enough to capture a leadership position or to introduce subsequent waves of improved products and services.

6

DISRUPTION, GLOBALIZATION, AND INNOVATION MANAGEMENT

Management literature is filled with examples of the changes wrought on business by the addition of technology and the creation of entirely new businesses whose primary product or service is technology. These changes have become of vital interest to companies who see technology as a means to improving their operations. They are also important to the inventors and vendors of this technology, encouraging them to identify the next product or service that customers will flock to. The term "killer app" is often used to describe the most wildly successful technologies or products. In the past, such killer apps have been the personal computer, laptop computer, personal digital assistant, Windows Operating System, word processor, Internet, electronic mail, World Wide Web, web browser, information portal, cellular telephone, and wireless messaging. Each of these has been so widely adopted that the leading providers have risen to the pinnacle of commercial success. Companies such as Microsoft, Dell Computers, Palm, Research in Motion, Yahoo, Google, and Nokia have all risen from obscurity to international prominence on the back of a killer app.

Three Major Trends

The power that technology brings to an organization has the potential to launch new ventures to global prominence and overturn established incumbents. Therefore, success in implementing or creating new technologies has become a topic of intense interest. Below are three major trends in the integration of technology and information into an organization.

1. Disruptive Impact of Technology

As technology has become a new tool for executing business functions, the optimization of these capabilities has opened a new domain for companies to achieve a competitive advantage in their industry. The ability to identify current sales and inventory levels has led to real-time supply systems. Information on credit card transactions contains clues that can identify fraudulent usage in near real-time. The military's ability to access real-time information about enemy movements and positions from anywhere in the world allows them to control all major confrontations.

Christensen (1997) illustrates the early emergence of technology transformation in earth excavation equipment from the 1920's to the mid-1950's. In the 1920's, only cable driven shovels possessed the power and leverage necessary to meet the needs of major construction projects. In 1947, the first hydraulically powered shovel was introduced in Britain and rapidly copied in America. This equipment was called the "backhoe" because it was small enough to attach to the back of farm equipment. The hydraulic seals in the equipment could support only a ¼ cubic yard bucket. Therefore, the backhoe was relegated to small farm and residential projects and posed no threat to the large construction jobs handled by cable driven shovels that could extract 4 cubic yards of earth in a bucket.

However, advances in seals and pumps soon led to hydraulic equipment that could handle larger buckets. By 1965, hydraulics could excavate 2 cubic yards per bucket and by 1974, over 10 cubic yards. These advances made hydraulics more powerful than the traditional cable powered excavators. This "disruptive innovation", as Christensen terms it, totally destroyed the cable excavation equipment industry and replaced it with a new group of companies that had developed hydraulic equipment. Christensen maintains that such technological advances will generate similar disruptions in every industry and he illustrates this with in-depth analysis of the steel and disk drive industries. The crux of Christensen's argument is illustrated in Figure 6.1. Upstart competitors can enter a market by serving low-profit margin customers. Because entrenched companies are more motivated to serve high-profit customers, they often cede the low-end to the upstart company. However, in an industry where technology can be applied to significantly improve product performance, the new entrant will move up market and attack the entire customer base of the entrenched company. This has occurred in a number of industries and has drawn the attention of business leaders around the world.

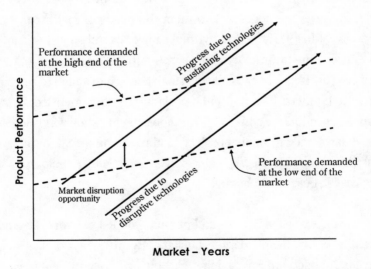

Figure 6.1 Disruptive Technological Change *(Christensen, 1997)*

In *The Innovator's Solution*, Christensen lists a number of technologies and companies that have overturned established industry leaders. These include Amazon.com, Bloomberg LP, Canon, Cisco, eBay, Federal Express, Intuit, Google, Intel, and RIM (Christensen, 2003). Each of these used emerging technologies to gain a small position in the market and then relied on the advancement of their technology to elevate them past long-entrenched leaders; significantly disrupting the industry.

Industry competition is no longer dominated solely by historical presence or financial size. The rapid advancement of technology is a lever that can be used to enter a market and move to a dominant position.

2. Technology Globalization

The second trend is the emergence of global competence to provide competitive products and services. Though a technology may be born in the United States, it can easily migrate to any country that is prepared to adopt it and invest in improvements and applications. The transistor was invented at Bell Labs, and RCA spent millions attempting to improve its properties to replace vacuum tube radios. Sony, on the other hand, turned early transistors into small pocket radios with inferior sound quality. That product gave them a position in the radio market, but a low profit margin position against which RCA did not want to compete.However, transistors proved to be the future of all radio equipment, and Sony was able to ride its position in transistor radios to market dominance and to completely drive RCA out of the industry (Chandler, 2001).

Later in the century, the explosion of information technology in business led to the creation of a new type of service—the IT consultancy. Companies such as Electronic Data Systems, Accenture, Bearing

Point, and PricecoopersWaterhouse developed large IT service businesses based on those needs. But, just as technology-based products migrated from America to Japan in the 20th century, technology-based services are migrating to more affordable countries in the 21st century. These types of jobs require special knowledge and expertise, but in a form that is repetitive and teachable. The ability of entrepreneurs and universities in India, China, Puerto Rico, and Russia to train such people and organize businesses to provide these services at lower costs, has led to significant outsourcing of American IT jobs. Business Week estimates that there are currently 150,000 IT engineers in Bangalore, India, and that one third of all new IT development work by U.S.-based companies is being done in India (Kripalani, 2003). This transition is almost identical to that of the electronics industry from 1950 and 1980. The standardization of computer equipment and software interfaces, improved global telecommunications, and competitive educational programs provide all of the ingredients necessary to perform software development, IT back office services, and call center support from anywhere on the globe. Just as the Japanese were able to take over the electronics markets, the Indians and Chinese are in a position to take a major share of the IT services market. Consulting firm, A.T. Kearney, estimates that by 2008 over 500,000 financial service jobs will be outsourced to companies outside of the U.S. (Kripalani, 2003).

More recently, the trade press is emphasizing that some of these jobs are being pulled back into the United States. However, this is a temporary balancing measure driven by the fact that companies outsourced too much capability too soon. The IT services industry in emerging countries is using Christensen's disruptive innovation curve to attack the market at the low end. Over time, their expertise will increase and the entire IT service industry could be lost to India and

China, just as the entire electronics industry was lost to Japan in the last century.

Technology and information are tremendous leveling tools. They do not discriminate based on political ideology, ethnic origins, language, social class, geographic location, or corporate boundaries. Companies and countries that develop an internal, integrated learning base possess a competitive advantage that will allow them to dominate an industry (Chandler, 2001).

3. Innovation Management

The third trend that we present is the growing importance of innovation management. Both the companies that create and those that apply technology need a new form of management; one that optimizes an organization in motion rather than an organization at rest. Managers who have mastered the skills necessary to keep a production line operating or a telephone switch working, have not necessarily mastered the skills necessary to successfully evolve those operations. Ongoing business operations are usually about repetitive activities. They call for methods to systematize activities that are performed over and over every day. The process is static and the personnel are molded to fit the process.

Conversely, the management of innovation requires a process that is constantly changing and keeping people flexible so they can perform well in different situations every year. A static process cannot be defined to meet these needs and people cannot be molded into a single form. Instead, the manager must find methods to measure and improve performance, but allow the people to adapt their performance to emerging needs. Innovation Management is a way of empowering people, setting guidelines, and building networks that can drive a business to innovate and reinvent itself in the midst of a changing market.

Impact on Management Practice

These changes have had significant impacts on management practice. First, most functional organizations have had to find a way to integrate technology professionals into their operations and their professional communities. The earth excavation field can no longer be populated only by those who operate excavators. This community must now include people who create tools to make excavation more efficient. It must find a way to welcome people with entirely different skill sets and unique perspectives on a problem.

Valuable resources are no longer limited to the four walls of the company's facilities. A team may include people throughout the company, within partner organizations, and across national boundaries. A team is less likely to be a homogeneous group and more likely to require an appreciation for the perspectives and traditions of a much broader set of people.

The executive ranks had previously been dominated by three major titles; the CEO, COO, and CFO. Together, they determined the direction of the company and assumed responsibility for its financial health, operational capability, and service to shareholders. But as technology has become a major ingredient in all operations, the executive ranks have been joined by others with special responsibilities for internal IT, product research, corporate knowledge, and information security. Companies now count the CIO (information), CTO (technology), CKO (knowledge), and CSO (security or strategy) as important members of the executive team.

Innovation Management

Technical applications that are propelling business, government, and military operations are developed by creative, intelligent, and inventive individuals and organizations. To some degree, the velocity of a significant part of the economy rests on the shoulders of these visionaries. The speed with which they innovate has a direct impact on the ability of their customers to integrate these new tools and improve their business performance. Opportunities that are lost in these technology companies represent potential lost improvements across a large sector of the world economy. Therefore, the optimization of innovation and creation is an important economic and business topic. The ability to innovate and create is essential, but the fruits of that ability cannot be realized without the ability to manage that innovation. To quote Henry Chesbrough, *"Technology by itself has no single objective value. The economic value of a technology remains latent until it is commercialized in some way"* (Chesbrough, 2003).

The ability to successfully manage innovation is one key to the success of companies such as Dell, GE, and Microsoft. In some cases, innovation is synonymous with research. In others, it is the application of existing ideas to new problems. GE's research labs practice innovation when they create new synthetic materials to improve medical implants. Microsoft practices innovation when it embeds search technology into its operating systems. In both cases, the companies recognize that the future is not a copy of the past and that they must take aggressive action to remain in their dominant position.

High Stakes

Alfred North Whitehead said, *"The greatest invention of the nineteenth century was the invention of the method for invention"* (Buderi, 2000). The 19th century saw a major transformation away from a reliance on independent scientists and inventors as the source of innovation and toward the creation of internal research labs and product development teams. Buderi (2000) describes the emergence of the German organic dye industry from the explorations of individual scientists to the establishment of corporate research staffs under the oversight of brilliant scientists. Companies such as Perkins, Bayer, BASF, Höchst, and AGFA all emerged in the 19th century and built their entire business on the products of their research laboratories.

In the 20th century, RCA enjoyed a near monopoly on radio technology and rode that position from 1919 to 1980. But business historian Alfred Chandler attributes RCA's downfall in the industry to its lack of an "internal learning base". The company controlled the critical patents for radio technology, but did not have the in-house expertise to develop new products and push that technology into new markets. Therefore, it was vulnerable to Japanese companies such as Matsushita and Sony, as they created new electronic products based on the transistor (Chandler, 2001).

Today, the same effect can be seen in computers, software, and Internet services. The world's preferred search engine shifts as new competitors release better technologies and word of it spreads like wildfire through the Internet. Search engine leaders such as Alta Vista and Yahoo were completely eclipsed when Google emerged from a Stanford research project.

Objectives

The primary objective of innovation management is to arrive at marketable products or services before a competitor does. As Chesbrough pointed out, it is the commercial application of technology, not just the creation of technology that defines successful innovation. James McGroddy, the head of the IBM T.J. Watson Research Center, realized the importance of this connection as early as 1989, when he observed that the research center had five Nobel Prize winners on its staff, but *"research was not making much difference to the company"* (Buderi, 2000).

New technology is born with great potential. In fact, the promises inherent in a technology always exceed society's ability to absorb, adopt, or apply it (Chakravorti, 2003). Innovation management seeks to identify that portion of the technology that is most amenable to the current social and market situation. It seeks to push forward applications that might become the next killer app and maintain the company's leading edge or propel it to the front of the pack at the expense of the current leader.

Action

Most academics and practitioners are familiar with the story of the Xerox Palo Alto Research Center (PARC), which, though very successful at creating innovations for the photocopier industry, lost its lead and its own technologies in the emerging computer industry (Smith, 1999 and Buderi, 2002). In the wake of this missed opportunity, companies are seeking new business models to insure that they capture the full value of their own innovations.

Starting Innovation. The first step in this procedure must always be starting the process of innovation. Any organization with a sufficient budget can create an innovation or research department, but that is not sufficient enough to succeed at the process. Markides (2002) maintains that beginning this process requires redefining the business. If the company's definition of itself remains the same, there is no place for innovation, change, and unique action. He recommends that a company redefine the answers to the following questions:

* Who is our customer?
* What products or services are we offering these customers?
* How can we offer better products or a new way of doing business with our customers?
* What are our unique capabilities?

After beginning with these questions, a company is ready to move on to establishing a management process for driving innovation.

The Best People. In considering an invitation to join the new Microsoft Research in 1993, Linda Stone's reaction was, *"Wow. I could come in to work every day and work with this group of people"* (Buderi, 2000). It was the amazing group of leading researchers that compelled her to accept the offer and put aside her previous opinions of the Redmond, Washington, company. Great innovation requires great people. The staff of the government's Manhattan Project, Lockheed's Skunk Works, and Apple's Macintosh computer, all drew upon the very special abilities of carefully selected people. Warren Bennis studied these and other projects and created a list of requirements for organizing geniuses to achieve great objectives. His list of 15 characteristics is dominated by the need for great people. In his words, the need is for "superb people", a "strong leader", "mission focus", talent that can work together, and "optimism" (Bennis, 1997).

The right processes, equipment, and mission cannot compensate for the wrong set of people. In some cases, the need is for technical knowledge; in others, creativity, the ability to organize, and the gift of motivation.

Tenets of Innovation. Arun Netravali, former president of Bell Labs, maintains that all successful research follows three tenets— speed, complexity, and cannibalization (Buderi, 2000). Research must move fast in its pursuit of advances. Reaching the goal one month or one year after the competition is almost as bad as not reaching the goal at all. That work may lay important groundwork for the next innovation, but it will have lost most of its commercial value to its faster rival.

In the real world, there are no ideal laboratory conditions. The unique value in an innovation often stems from its ability to handle the complexity that exists in business operations. Computer switching equipment from Lucent must be able to deal with a wide variety of signal speeds and computer systems from a number of vendors. An innovation for the fastest switch for a single signal and computer combination is not nearly as valuable as a less than optimal switch that can work effectively with all combinations of signals and equipment in the network.

Finally, a research organization must obsolete its own products, services, processes, and organizational structures. It must push for innovation and improvement even at the expense of its existing products and services. If an organization does not cannibalize its own products, then a competitor will. Intel Corporation is famous for this type of behavior. The last version of their CPU is just becoming a market staple when the company releases the next generation that significantly surpasses it. But, if Intel did not do this to its own products, AMD would.

Cannibalization and speed are necessary partners in the innovation process.

Value Extraction. At Xerox PARC in the 1980's, the value of all research was measured by the degree to which it contributed to a complete system that could be sold into a client organization. Up to that time, this process had served it well in creating new technologies for its photocopier products. However, as its research created technologies more useful in computing and communications, it was the wrong metric for identifying the value inherent in the technology itself. As a result, a number of researchers left Xerox to start their own companies and were able to license the technology for a small price. Xerox hoped that the success of those technologies would stimulate sales of their existing products, and therefore, did not seek major ownership positions in the spin-offs.

This process led to the creation of over 20 new companies focused on computer hardware and software. The most successful of these have been 3Com and Adobe, followed by a number that were reacquired once they had proven their value in the market (Chesbrough, 2003).

Viewing this as a lesson in value extraction, major players like IBM, Intel, and Lucent have created new methods for managing technologies from their laboratories. Like Xerox, IBM initially viewed itself as a complete system provider and sought to develop technologies that would improve its major systems. But in recent years, it has changed that model and begun to extract value in different ways. Its first major change was to become a system integrator of standard computer components—the birth of the IBM personal computer. From there, it moved into IT services that were not limited to IBM computer products. These services competed directly with EDS and consulting firms like Accenture and Bearing Point. More recently it has decided to extract value through technology licensing.Its 2½" hard drive technology has become a staple in a number of vendors' laptop computers. Though the technology was originally developed to give a competitive advantage to IBM's ThinkPad line of laptops, the company has sold as many hard drives to other vendors as it has sold ThinkPad laptops. This has doubled the company's revenues for the drives.IBM has begun licensing its intellectual property and allows other companies to build hardware based on its unique IP. Finally, IBM has started a program entitled First of a Kind (FOAK), in which it explores a new and unproven technology in conjunction with a major customer. Both participants contribute their own resources and successful technologies become IBM IP, which supports future innovation (Chesbrough, 2003). This value extraction is considerably more complex than the typical 1980's era practices at PARC, Watson, and Bell labs.

Intel spent $3.8 billion on innovation in 2001. With such a large investment, the company must do everything it can to extract the maximum value from this innovation. One extremely successful practice has been their "Copy Exactly" policy. Chip development and production facilities are constructed as exact copies of each another. Both use the same machinery, models, and configuration settings to produce their chips. The layout of the production line is identical, as are the processes for operating the system. This insures that the newly developed chips and the production line chips will have exactly the same characteristics. The productivity levels in the development facility are identical to the productivity levels that will be achieved in production. This process has saved significant time and cost in selling customers, receiving production approvals, and migrating new processes and equipment into the production environment.

Intel also improves their value extraction by establishing research partnerships with universities and consortia, and then managing them closely. Contrary to the more common practice of giving money to a university and allowing it to pursue its own path, Intel assigns engineers to work directly with the students so they have the advantage of the most current level of knowledge and can advance more quickly. Intel has also established a venture capital organization that funds external companies—which it works closely with to improve their productivity and effectiveness.

Organizational Process. The actual organizational process for an innovative group appears to be less unique than the characteristics described above. These processes are defined in a number of texts, one of these being *Radical Innovation* (Leiffer et al, 2000). With the cooperation of ten major research organizations, including GE, GM, IBM, and DuPont, the authors attempted to identify a process that has been most effective for managing innovation and turning innovative ideas into products. The result was a list of the following essential activities.

1. *Market Learning.* Instill a mindset of constant market learning. Use large, small, formal, and informal sampling to extract information. Be open to counter-intuitive information. Tap into User Innovation Communities. Examples of these include the Open Source software movement, homebrew computer makers, kit airplanes, telephone "phreaking", computer virus underground, amateur game developers, and "monster garage" mechanics (von Hippel, 2002 and Thomke, 2003)

2. *Find a Place in the Value Chain.* Map technical innovation to business success. Every innovation must demonstrate that is has value to the company. The value extraction practices of the IBM T.J. Watson Research Center described above illustrate this process very well.

3. *Effectively Build Business Models.* Understand the value chain and how the company plays in that chain. Modify the business model to incorporate innovative products. Prepare for war with established business units.

4. *Fight for Funding.* Every innovation team should include an expert in resource acquisition. Senior management must balance investments in innovation against investments in current operations. Innovation projects must win these decision-makers to their side. Seek sources of external funding.

5. *Build Partnerships.* Modern products and services often require more resources than exist within a single organization. Build partnerships with other companies without jeopardizing the internal value of the innovation.

6. *Transition to a Business Unit.* Establish a transition team and write a transition plan. Recruit senior managers as transition champions. Invest in transition, just as you did in innovation. Successful transition is a key part of successful innovation.

7. *Managing Individuals.* Balance the composition of the innovation team. Include people with skills beyond intelligence. Retaining talented people in a risky environment requires investment

and long-range planning. Contract for specialized help outside of the team. Transition personnel as you transition innovation.

This process has proven useful at a number of large organizations. Small companies may find it difficult to implement or finance. However, the flowering of the venture capital community has made it possible for even small start-ups to deploy significant capital toward their innovation process.

Conclusion

Technology and information management is much more than just installing, optimizing, and operating IT systems within an organization. Technology has become a central feature of nearly every business and has the power to significantly influence its market success. Effective management of the innovation process is an essential step in structuring and building a company in the 21st century. Without success in this area, competitors will move aggressively through the market and displace companies that are not innovating; that are standing still as Alta Vista and RCA stood still in the 20th century.

7

HOW LONG
DOES IT MATTER?

usiness, society, and the world are all on an evolutionary track. Each member and group is competing for some form of dominance over the others. In the 1990's, the introduction of information technology (IT) into business operations created a significant spike in the capabilities of companies that managed to incorporate it in a useful way. They took an evolutionary step in efficiency. IT is not the first innovation to have had this effect and it will not be the last. However, while we are in the midst of the explosion, it is very difficult to predict the top of the performance improvement curve and the beginning of diminishing returns. This is what Nicholas Carr attempted to do with his Harvard Business Review article (Carr, 2003) and his subsequent book (Carr, 2004a).

Carr broadly questioned the continuing ability of IT to provide companies with a competitive advantage over their competitors. He argued that, like previous innovations, IT must transition from a source of competitive advantage to an integrated component of every business. This statement, and his prediction that this turning point had already come, provoked a phalanx of attacks from IT industry executives and created an ongoing media debate that has not completely subsided nearly two years later.

Emergence of IT Advantage

IT has its roots in the beginnings of the computer industry and the emergence of the Internet as business tools. Initially, both of these technologies were experiments into what could be accomplished. Their early applications were in very specialized fields that required computing power, like the analysis of nuclear weapon effects, or problems that needed long-distance reliable communications, like military command and control. However, as these technologies became more affordable and more accessible, other businesses began to apply them to every form of industry. Companies gradually discovered the best approaches for leveraging these IT systems toward improved production efficiencies, rapid information exchange, meaningful staff reductions, and additional new inventions—each of which proved to be a competitive advantage. However, IT is not a proprietary technology. It is a publicly available product that can be purchased by any company that can afford the price. Therefore, advantages achieved through computer controlled milling machines are soon copied by other companies, until everyone in the industry is performing more efficiently. IT lifts all companies that adopt it, while those who do not, sink to the bottom and lose their relevance.

Since a company cannot defend, control, or hide IT from its competitors, it cannot retain a long-term monopoly on any advantages gained from it. Carr argues that the advantages are temporary and are lost over time. Early adopters realize some benefits at the beginning. With experience, they are able to increase these benefits through improvements in implementation and by finding the places where IT has the most leverage. However, as competitors adopt this same technology, the relative advantage of one company over another diminishes. Therefore, after reaching some peak, the advantage decreases until it is a very small part of the business. In this sense, the advantages gained may follow a Poisson distribution as shown in Figure 7.1. Like the Poisson distribution, the advantages gained never recede completely to zero. Small advantages can be gained through IT system improvements, wise selection of competing products, and good timing on new purchases and implementations. However, the lion's share of the advantage is in the past and will not be repeated.

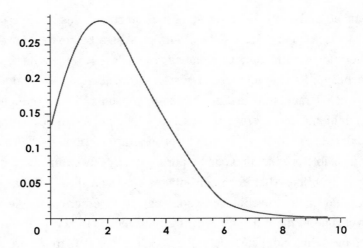

Figure 7.1 Poisson Distribution for Competitive Advantage

Decline of the IT Advantage

The crux of Carr's argument is not that this transition happens for all innovations, but that it has already occurred for IT. He suggests that the early adopters have discovered the most powerful ways to extract value from IT for business activities and that these methods have been copied across the industry. Therefore, IT is already becoming ubiquitous and providing correspondingly less advantage to those who use it. Carr illustrates this with the S verses Z-curves shown in Figure 7.2. His argument is that we are certainly in the central region labeled "Diminishing advantage" and may even be getting close to the right-hand side of "Weak advantages".

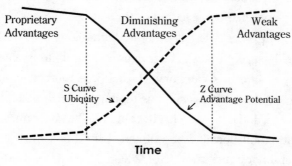

Evolution of Business Technology

Copyright 2004 by Nicholas G. Carr

Figure 7.2 S-curve of Ubiquity vs. Z-curve of Advantage *(Carr, 2004b)*

The ubiquity of the technology is the source of its own downfall in providing an advantage, but this is also its strength as an enduring ingredient within business. A similar path has been followed by the steam engine, railroad, telegraph, telephone, and electricity generation. All of these have become an integral part of world industry. None of them would be considered optional (assuming that the telegraph is the grandfather to the Internet), though none are considered a unique source of competitive advantage to the companies that use them because every competitor has access to them as well. Lumping IT into the same "old" category as electricity has drawn criticism from across the IT industry. Robert Metcalfe, inventor of Ethernet, is one of those leaders who have challenged Carr's position (Metcalfe, 2004). However, like many other IT defenders, Metcalfe does not really address the question of whether IT has reached its peak in providing competitive advantage. Instead, he points out that IT sales are still strong, companies still need the products, and vendors continue to create better products for these customers. He seems to miss the entire connection to competitive advantage and focuses instead, on revenue generation. Andy Grove, legendary Chairman of Intel, does understand what Carr is saying. He agrees that basic transaction processing has crossed the second arc in the S-curve and is a mature technology around the world. However, he disagrees that all IT services and computer-based systems can be lumped into this category. He believes there is considerable room for innovation in areas such as digital music, digital telephones, wireless access, and data search. He contends that Carr attracted such a flood of attention because he published the book during the third year of a technology recession (Hof, 2003).

The competitive advantage of innovation faces a number of staged reductions, and, as Grove pointed out, we may have witnessed only one of those steps down. Reduction may follow a smooth curve as the innovation propagates through a regional industry, but this may be followed by a sharp drop when local successes are copied throughout an entire country's industry. It may then decrease gradually as the efficiency of IT adoptions improves. Then, it will face another precipice when the innovation is adopted by countries with a similar socio-economic status to the originator. This pattern may repeat itself as the technology becomes accessible to countries further down the developmental ladder. Working its way down this ladder is difficult at the beginning because an innovation often requires significant technical expertise to implement and operate it. When this expertise is available in limited numbers, it is controlled by the country with the most money. Only as the expertise pool grows, can other countries afford to hire the people necessary to implement the innovation. There is also another force in the commoditization of an innovation. Barriers to adoption represent opportunities which entrepreneurs are eager to capitalize on. They recognize that making a technology more accessible will create a new customer-base—customers that they are eager to capture. Therefore, in addition to creating powerful tools, there is a strong motivation to create tools that are more accessible. All of this has occurred and continues to occur within IT.

Inevitable Ubiquity

The end goal, according to Carr, is for IT to become boring. Like electricity, it will become fully integrated and largely reliable in all industries and most countries. When this happens, companies must turn to other sources of competitive advantage. Has this already happened in IT? It appears that the powerful computing and communication technologies are already accessible to everyone who needs them, and there is sufficient expertise available to implement anything that needs implementing. In the defense simulation and analysis industry these power technologies are:

* Desktop computing,
* Word processing,
* Project management tools,
* Electronic mail,
* Internet access,
* Secure web-based data exchange,
* High-power computing,
* Graphics rendering power, and
* Computerized accounting, billing, and record keeping.

There are a number of other technologies that are useful, but provide much smaller improvements. Some that are vying for funding right now are:

- Cellular Internet access (like Blackberry) and
- Customer Relationship Management.

In the back-office application of IT for transaction processing, it may indeed have lost its power to convey advantage. However, we are still equipped with a fantastically powerful tool in the computer and the Internet. New applications emerge around the edges of mainstream business all the time, such as digital music sharing, data search, and peer-to-peer computing. However, when riding the technology S-curve (Figure 7.3), it is always important to recognize when it is time to get off a maturing technology, like IT services, and onto the next exploding opportunity, like RFID or nanotechnology.

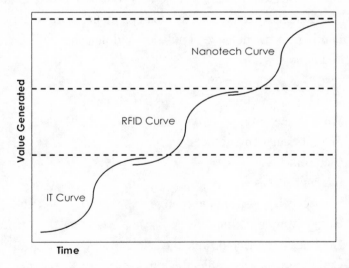

Figure 7.3 Riding the Technology S-curves

8

GOVERNMENT CTO

overnment organizations have a long and rich history of leading explorations into new technologies. From the Manhattan Project to the Space program, government scientists and managers have created some of the largest breakthroughs in technology ever made. Today much of the technology work has been outsourced to commercial industry, but government organizations that oversee this work continue to include world-class scientists, engineers, and mathematicians. These technologists guide the evolution of existing products and press for revolutionary solutions to increasingly complex problems.

Some of these technologists hold the title of Chief Technology Officer. This position usually allows them to focus on the technical aspects of problems and solutions, leaving specific management, administrative, and contractual details to others in the organization. These CTOs have a huge impact on the adoption of new technologies and research into new ideas. Given that a great deal of new technology in the last two decades has been in the form of computers and information systems, it is not surprising that for some organizations, the CTO can become nearly synonymous with the CIO. However, from a broader perspective, the CTO has very unique responsibilities that are focused on technology that may include computers, composite materials, rocket motors, medicines, and new forms of energy.

In this article, we profile several government CTOs and extract lessons from the work that they are doing to advance the national state-of-technology in defense, city and county government, services to citizens, and administrative oversight. These lessons focus on the government's responsibilities in technology:

* Integration,
* Architecture,
* Reuse and Duplication,
* Innovation, and
* Technology Policy.

Dawn Meyerriecks, DISA

Dawn Meyerriecks is the CTO for the Defense Information Systems Agency (DISA). This agency is responsible for the command and control computers throughout the military. It develops global networks that allow military personnel worldwide to share information that is essential to conducting their missions. As the CTO, she works with everyone in the 1,200-person organization to ensure that they are taking advantage of the right technologies and getting these fielded efficiently. This includes encryption, biometrics, and wireless technology to support classified systems and operations.

After earning a degree in Electrical Engineering at Carnegie Mellon University, she joined defense contractor TRW, then moved to the Jet Propulsion laboratories, and finally, to DISA. Her education and career in technology began in the late 1970's, when women in engineering and computer science were rare. However, over the years, she says this has changed and DISA now has women throughout its ranks.

Though working as a computer programmer was extremely rewarding and enjoyable, Meyerriecks' climb to the CTO position required that she "give up the keyboard" and focus more on working with people. Today, her effectiveness is measured by her ability to get large numbers of people working together toward a common goal. This can be extremely difficult within the Department of Defense where individual services—the Army, Navy, Air Force, and Marine Corps—can all behave as fiefdoms that refuse to cooperate. The Defense Information System Agency must create common computing and communications solutions that bridge these service boundaries and enable these groups to work together on the battlefield, in spite of their differences. To accomplish this, Meyerriecks models her leadership style on that of her predecessor, former Technical Director, Frank Perry; who is now CTO with the Department of Veterans Affairs. *"I learned don't ever let anybody know they're getting to you,"* she says. *"If you can maintain calm when everyone around you is angry or frightened, they will look to you."* She recognizes that her leverage comes from reason, dependability, and receptiveness towards the concerns of others. A CTO who can do this effectively is much more valuable to the organization than someone who attempts to impose standards by edict; without discussion and consideration. In this respect, Dawn Meyerriecks has made a huge jump in her ability to powerfully influence the development of military information systems.

Meyerriecks wrestles with both technical and cultural challenges within DISA and DoD. Technically she is searching for new methods to allow DoD to achieve interoperability across many families of communications and computing systems. Achieving this requires bringing service sponsors to standards that are not service-specific or even DoD specific. She must get the military to adopt commercial standards because commercial applications now move forward much faster than DoD solutions. Therefore, the military finds itself using commercial tools that operate on commercial standards.

Her office is also tackling the issue of managed identity and access control. Tens of thousands of military personnel access thousands of computer systems and networks every day. Each person has approval to access a different set of systems and the need to know limited sets of data. Establishing a practical system of identity verification that can be used in the field by people at all levels of technical expertise is a major challenge. To assist DISA with these issues, Meyerriecks' office has published a list of the major technical challenges that they face and would like industry help with. Providing this type of direction and solic- itation is an important part of the partnership that DISA has built with commercial vendors such as Microsoft, IBM, Oracle, and Verisign.

DISA's challenges are not just technical—they are also cultural. As described above, they are struggling to get all of the communities within the Department of Defense to accept common solutions to prob- lems, commercial standards, intellectual property from other services, and market forces. This is a very different approach to the tradition of relying on government policy for all decisions. These types of is- sues must often be tackled hand-in-hand with the technical issues. It is often impossible to separate things like commercial standards from the policies and historical precedents for opposing such standards that have built up within the organization over decades. To some degree, "commonality" across the Army, Navy, and Air Force diminishes the independence, unique identity, and tradition of these groups. DISA and Meyerriecks must build cooperation, commonality, and standardiza- tion within computer and communication systems, without diminish- ing the spirit of uniqueness that is cherished by each military branch.

Finally, Meyerriecks is trying to implement the IT side of the mil- itary's conversion to "Network-centric Warfare". Her office has expressed this as a change from "command and control" to "command and coordination". DoD and DISA recognize that computer systems and modern weapons allow people to operate more independently and to be more effective. Therefore, they are attempting to replace some of the "control" that has been typical of military operations with "coordination". We can no longer control everything that happens in a military operation. Our modern systems allow us to release some of that control to automated systems and empowered leaders. The goal then becomes to coordinate their actions toward the overall mission. This is very different from the traditional doctrine of control and subordination. Groups like the Army Rangers, Navy SEALS, and Marine Expeditionary Forces, blazed the trail on coordination of individual initiative and decision-making. The modern political situation calls for the employment of more forces of this type and fewer of the mechanized armies of World War II. Therefore, this culture and the weapons to empower it, are propagating throughout the military.

Melody Mayberry-Stewart, City of Cleveland, Ohio

Dr. Melody Mayberry-Stewart, Chief Technology Officer for the City of Cleveland, is responsible for developing, implementing, and supporting Information Technology (IT) strategies to improve government services for the City. Her challenge is to produce an IT-savvy government that uses the latest technology to be *operational, efficient, and effective*.

A native Clevelander, Chief Mayberry-Stewart is the founder and CEO of the Black Diamond IT Consulting Group. She has more than 25 years of IT experience and works with CEOs, COOs, and CIOs to develop IT strategy, and build high-performance IT organizations to improve organizational performance. She was the first African American female General Manager and Vice President of Corporate and Shared Services, for worldwide delivery of IT systems and operations for the BP Amoco Corporation, where she had global responsibility for the design and implementation of IT systems and services. Prior to joining BP Amoco, Mayberry-Stewart was the first and only Black female Chief Information Officer (CIO) in the health care industry in the country. She was the CIO at Beth Israel Medical Center, with headquarters in New York City, earning more than $1 billion in revenues annually.

The City of Cleveland relies on Mayberry-Stewart to lead efforts to modernize its information infrastructure. The old infrastructure evolved as a number of disparate and incompatible systems. Through competitive contracting, the city has selected SBS Communications to design and deploy a new system that ties together all of the city services and makes them more accessible to the citizens.

Mayberry-Stewart inherited a city that had very poor technology penetration. Only 25% of city employees had access to email, governmental IT positions were staffed with minimally qualified individuals, and IT positions carried sub-standard pay levels, making it difficult to attract highly qualified candidates. She has been working with the city's Director of Finance to access the financial resources needed to fix this situation. However, she recognizes that technology systems must compete with other departments for the same limited pool of resources. They are constantly balancing purchases between new police cars, construction new of water processing plants, and upgrades to the IT infrastructure. She presents cities like Honolulu, Chicago, and Seattle as models for the capabilities she is targeting. One of her most important missions is working with city council to educate them to the economic and social benefits of IT, and hopefully winning their support.

Case Western Reserve University has led the creation of the One-Cleveland organization, to bring together non-profit and government agencies that can build a communications infrastructure within the city. Their goal is to promote education, training, cultural events, and access to government services for the population of Cleveland. This network will support the needs of schools, museums, hospitals, police and fire departments, and government offices, to access high-speed networks for better internal operations and service to citizens. Through OneC-leveland's efforts, each of these organizations will not have to build or purchase their own backbone infrastructure between their facilities, but will be able to leverage a common backbone supporting all city servic-es. Mayberry-Stewart represents the interests of the City of Cleveland within this group, and provides expertise and insight into the needs of the city and the local government's plans to meet those needs.

Mike Macedonia, Army Simulation, Training, and Instrumentation

Mike Macedonia served as the CTO for the Army's Program Exec-utive Office for Simulation, Training, and Instrumentation (PEO STRI) for six years. His organization is responsible for creating everything from 3D immersive tank simulators to advanced laser-tag systems for use in the California desert. STRI uses the latest computers and net-working equipment to create realistic training devices and scenarios that can teach soldiers what war is going to be like, and prepare them to succeed long before they have to go into harm's way. Macedonia says, *"Our soldiers are virtual veterans before they even go into conflict ... we take them to the edge and let them know that they are going to do alright [in combat]."*

To assist STRI in building these systems, Dr. Macedonia has to explore new technologies and build partnerships both inside and outside of government. He is constantly exploring the capabilities of new graphics chips, new techniques in artificial intelligence for soldier behavior, and advances in computer games. This latter subject has landed Macedonia and STRI in the popular media a number of times. They have worked with game development companies including There Inc. and Pandemic Studios, to create game-like systems that also have the ability to teach soldiers to do their jobs better. Though computer games like Unreal and Quake have many of the same appearances of military simulations, the presence of anti-gravity devices, teleporters, and rail guns are not conducive to teaching soldiers to use their equipment effectively in real combat. But, the raw materials are there to create more realistic environments and military training devices that can accomplish this. Projects like Full Spectrum Warrior for the X-box, leverage advances in commercial games to create a realistic training system. Macedonia has also worked with There Inc. to create a massive multiplayer environment that can bring together teams of soldiers from around the globe to train with each other and exchange ideas.

Dr. Macedonia earned his Ph.D. from the Naval Postgraduate School under Mike Zyda, a leader in interactive computer graphics. Prior to that, he also served as an Army infantry officer during Desert Storm. Macedonia understands both the real-world and the virtual-world views of Army missions. Looking into the future, Macedonia recognizes that all future recruits will have grown up with computer and console games. Therefore, the Army must learn to communicate and teach them through this medium in the same way that the Army of WWII used Disney Animation Studios to create educational movies for the soldiers. Today, no one questions the value of educational movies, but the move into computer gaming required moving that perspective into the future; to focus on a medium that future soldiers will have grown up with.

To assist in its quest to create the ultimate training environment, the PEO STRI has created its own research and development organization at the University of Southern California. The Institute for Creative Technology (ICT) was created by a $50 million grant to the university with the stated objective *"to create a liaison between the service and the entertainment industry, for the purpose of enhancing simulation-based training."* The result has been a number of innovative products, including the Alternative Leadership Training Simulation, Full Spectrum Warrior, and Flatworld. Each of these products pushes the Army beyond the edge of current technology and creates new solutions that were not previously reachable.

Prior to World War II, a little known inventor working in his father's organ factory had created a very sophisticated flight simulator. However, he was unable to interest the Army Air Corps in the devices, so he sold them to amusement parks and continued to develop the technology. When the war started, there was a sudden need to rapidly train hundreds of pilots, and the Army was eager to buy the leading edge flight simulators created by Edwin Link in Binghamton, New York. In both the 1940's and the 2000's, the newest, advanced simulator technology was available to the public for entertainment before it became a military training product. Today, we harvest computer hardware and software from the gaming industry just as we did from the arcades of the past—and we look to the CTO's of organizations like PEO STRI to provide the vision to do it.

Frank Perry, Veterans Affairs

Frank Perry, the CTO at the Office of Veterans Affairs, occupies a position that reports directly to the CIO of the office. In providing services to the office and to the huge number of veterans around the country, the VA found that it needed someone to focus on the technology behind the IT systems being deployed, while the CIO focused on policy decisions and the best serves that the office should provide. Prior to hiring Perry, the VA found that they were falling further and further behind in understanding and deploying the new technologies being offered by industry. They needed someone to remain abreast of these advances and keep the CIO informed on what was available and what was doable.

Free of the political relationships, capital planning, and intra-agency communication required of the CIO, the CTO was able to master the technologies involved and guide the implementation of technology in the most efficient manner possible. *"The CIO has become business-driven first and technology-driven second,"* said Dawn Meyerriecks, CTO for DISA. *"Agencies need a CTO to understand the trends and be the principle technologist who will be around for a long time."*

Tom Berray, executive director at Cabot Consultants Inc., an executive search firm in McLean, Va., said *"most CTOs fit into one of two models; those that run an agency's day-to-day operations and those that*

*figure out how to use technology to change the way the government works
with its customers."*

Norman Lorentz, Office of Management and Budget

Lorentz returned to federal government following the incidents of
9/11 because he was "really pissed off" and wanted to work on the
problem. He was serving as a Senior VP at recruiting firm Dice.com
and had previously served as the CTO of the US Postal Service. The
Office of Management and Budget created its own CTO position to allow Lorentz to work on the Federal Enterprise Architecture, under the
leadership of Mark Forman, OMB CIO.

Lorentz is credited with reinvigorating the Architecture and Infrastructure Committee within the CIO Council. This committee was responsible for creating the widely applied Federal Enterprise Architecture that creates a structure for all IT implementations across OMB
and many other government offices.

One of his goals was to bring the CTO out of pure technology implementation and into mission-related decision-making. This is a responsibility similar to that of the CTOs in industry. Just as Pat Gelsinger, CTO at
Intel Corp., is actively involved in directing the company's strategic use of
technology, Lorentz was hoping to allow the leading technologist within
OMB to contribute to the decision-making process for the entire office.

Another of his responsibilities is the reduction of duplication within
OMB and across a number of other federal agencies. Such a position
is fraught with disagreement and protection of existing programs. Just

as he has done at USPS, and as his predecessor, Robert Otto is doing now, Lorentz will seek out opportunities to consolidate operations and eliminate waste. Otto has said that, *"The most basic element of the consolidation has been the centralization of the Postal Service's servers. From an IT infrastructure that included 15,000 servers at hundreds of locations across the country, the agency has whittled the number down to 3,000 servers at two IT centers; in Eagan, Minn., and San Mateo, Calif. The move has saved the agency $30 million a year."*

Likewise, he has reduced the number of staff members' software tools from 1,500 to 380, the number of vendor partners from 200 to a dozen, and the number of help desks from 119 to four. He said he plans to eventually have just one help desk for the entire operation.

Conclusion

The cases presented above illustrate some of the important responsibilities of a technology executive in government service. These responsibilities are unique from those of the corporate world, since the government usually operates in an over-site role for a number of programs being executed by government contractors. The government CTO must be sufficiently technical and current to accurately evaluate the claims and progress of the contractors. But, this person must also provide the technical vision to the government office, which can define where it will go in the future, what it wants to provide to its customers/constituents, and what it can realistically request from industry.

The CTO position is not an industry-only responsibility. Business leaders and academics both agree that there is quickly becoming no company, organization, or endeavor that does not incorporate technology, and within which the effective management, application, and adoption of technology cannot improve organizational performance. Increasingly, government offices will encounter their own need for a technology executive and apply this person to their own organizational performance improvements, just as they have aggressively applied information technology over the last decade and created e-government services in recent years.

9

THE FEMALE CTO

In this enlightened time, most leaders recognize that women are capable of performing executive roles just as well as men. However, we find that men largely populate the position of the CTO. The degree to which men dominate this position is difficult to measure. In an attempt to quantify it, we turned to the Google Image Search engine and executed a search for "Chief Technology Officer". This returned over 4,000 images, many of them corporate mug shots of men and women wearing suits and serious expressions. We repeated this search multiple times spread over a period of several months. Interestingly, it returned a very similar album of photos each time. More specifically for this chapter, it returned the same set of photos of women CTOs every time. Among the first 200 mug shots, we found only eight that were women; and consistently, the same eight. This method of identifying the ratio between male and female CTOs leaves a great deal to be desired from a scientific perspective. But, it does reveal that female CTOs do exist, and are a small fraction of the CTO population. The search results indicate a ratio of 96% male to 4% female. The National Science Foundation reports that women form only 22% of the science and engineering workforce, though they are 42% of the overall workforce. It appears that the female CTO positions are far from the 22% female population in science and engineering.

As with all Google results, the eight female mug shots that appeared were accompanied by links to the web sites on which they resided. This provided a source of information on the identity, career, and background of these rare female CTOs, as well as a way to contact these women. In this chapter, we will explore the careers of several of these female CTOs—their origins, responsibilities, and accomplishments.

Google's Top Eight Female CTOs
• Dr. Lisa Bergman, CTO and co-Founder, Orielle Inc.
• Dr. Rita Schnipke, CTO, Blue Ridge Numerics Inc.
• Dawn Meyerriecks, CTO, Defense Information Systems Agency
• Mary Doyle, CTO and Vice President for Information Systems, Washington State University.
• Dr. Melody Mayberry-Stewart, CTO, City of Cleveland
• Rosalie Deane, CTO, Capital and Credit Merchant Bank
• Jane Janis, CTO, Information Institute of Syracuse
• Kristin Schnoebelen, CTO, D3 Inc.

Patterns of Eight Female CTOs

The nature of the organizations in which these women serve, largely determines the definition of the CTO position. In previous publications, we described the Five Patterns of the CTO. These patterns organize the most dominant responsibilities of CTOs in a diverse set of corporations, government agencies, and other organizations. Research into the companies and careers of the CTOs we are profiling, indicated which of these patterns each person fit into. These patterns provide a useful structure and generic definition for each of the women profiled in this chapter (Figure 9.1). It is encouraging to see that the female CTOs are spread across all of the patterns, and not stereotyped into a single role.

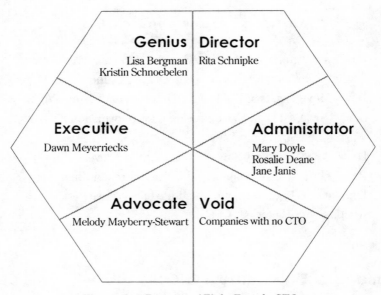

Figure 9.1 Patterns of Eight Female CTOs

Genius

The Genius Pattern describes a CTO who is the company's expert in a specific technical field, and is an active practitioner in, or creator of new technology to support the company's products and services. This CTO pattern is most often found in young start-up companies where one of the founders is the technical brain behind the operation. One famous example of this pattern, is the partnership between Steve Jobs and Steve Wozniak in creating Apple Computer. Jobs was the master of marketing and sales, while Wozniak was the genius that created the computers.

Dr. Lisa Bergman is an excellent example of this pattern of CTO. She is a faculty member in the Physics Department of the University of Idaho and simultaneously serves as the CTO of start-up company, Orielle. Peter Mills and Lisa Bergman started this company in 1999, in the Research Triangle of North Carolina. Their primary focus was in consulting services and research contracts for distributed computing, parallel algorithms, and data fusion. Mills' experience at Duke University and Applied Research Associates provided the background that he needed to start a new company. He joined with Bergman, whose expertise is in the physical and materials science, to create a company that could expand beyond its software origins. Recognizing the need for differentiation from hundreds of other software companies, Mills and Bergman are seeking to build a company that can offer research services in both the software and hardware domains.

Dr. Bergman's principle focus and contribution to the company is in the optical properties of semiconductors and quantum devices, as well as the photoluminescent spectroscopy necessary to image the fine details of these devices. This expertise allows Orielle to pursue small business innovative research (SBIR) contracts that are more complex than simply software applications. Many of today's mid-sized defense software and computer systems companies began in the same way, and Orielle is hoping to duplicate their success with their combination of information systems and physical sciences expertise.

When Orielle bids on defense SBIR contracts, Dr. Bergman provides the technical expertise necessary for the principle investigator of such projects. Her extensive expertise in semiconductor physics, applied mathematics, and the programming of numerical methods, allows the company to convince government agencies that they do have the expertise necessary to generate valuable research and new innovations that can be implemented in defense and civilian products.

Photoluminescent spectroscopy is an extremely specialized technology, but it is also a conduit into understanding and researching properties of semiconductors. This expertise may allow the company to dominate a very specialized technology niche. This niche will not support the growth of the next IBM or Intel, but it is an excellent way to create and establish a new small company. Orielle can build a reputation as the very best service provider in this field. This reputation can become the foundation for a strong and steady business, allowing the CTO to build relationships with government sponsors and partner companies. A reputation for successful innovation will allow Orielle to branch out into other adjacent fields and grow the base of expertise of the company. Mills has already expanded for specialized parallel computing software algorithms into the physical sciences; further movement into related fields is the growth trajectory for Orielle.

Becoming an expert in a small niche, is also an excellent strategy for positioning the company for acquisition. Dominating a field can lock larger companies out of that niche. When that technology becomes an essential part of a major product or service, larger companies often become very interested in bringing that capability in-house. Companies such as Intel, Google, Yahoo, Akamai, Lockheed Martin, Northrop Grumman, and hundreds of others, are constantly purchasing smaller companies that can help them solve larger system problems. If Mills and Bergman are willing to position their company for acquisition, their mastery of complex software algorithms and photoluminescent spectroscopy will provide a path to personal wealth, and perhaps a senior position in the acquiring company.

Lisa Bergman and Orielle are focusing on technical specialization as a strategy for growth and potential acquisition.

Director

The director pattern provides oversight and direction to a team of technologists, ensuring that the technology is aligned with the business vision. It emerged from the position of Director of R&D laboratories, which was the highest technical position within most companies up until the 1980's. These types of CTOs are often very technically competent, and may have served in the role of the genius CTO at one time. However, the growth of the company often demands that they turn the hands-on technical work over to others, to focus on broader leadership issues within the company and to promote the technical vision of the company.

Rita Schnipke's has had a rich career in the numerical analysis of data. She began as a scientist in the oil industry and moved into fluid flow and heat transfer software for industrial design and manufacturing. Her Ph.D. in mechanical and aerospace engineering certainly prepared her to serve as the genius CTO and a co-founder of Compuflow Inc. There, she worked to develop computation fluid dynamics software for corporate R&D customers; hard-core scientists who specialized in CFD and provided their services to manufacturing divisions. Compuflow competed with all of the other major vendors in CFD software, providing scientific products on Unix workstations. Their success led to acquisition by ANSYS in 1992.

Computational fluid dynamics (CFD) software is used to analyze the performance of mechanical parts in automobile engines, spacecraft, and other machinery. Though most people may not be familiar with the term "CFD", the media has often used images from this software to illustrate the buildup of heat and stress on systems like the space shuttle. These familiar rainbow colored images provide a beautiful depiction of the laws of physics at work.

Rita Schnipke and her partner, Ed Williams, recognized that the engineering and product design world needed an accessible software package for performing CFD. Existing tools were targeted at R&D organizations that provided their services to the designers working in a manufacturing facility. These required extensive expertise and specialized computers to perform the analysis. This work was so expensive and time consuming, that it was performed only on the finished designs for new parts and vehicles. This allowed the designers to modify the final design to avoid specific weaknesses, but it did not allow them to analyze dozens of prototype designs that were created much earlier in the process. Schnipke and Williams wanted to create a tool that this community could use themselves, to explore the properties of all of their early design concepts. Accomplishing this required rethinking the fundamental assumptions of the CFD software industry. They needed a software package that did not require an expert to operate it, and that could run on a much more common computer configuration. This vision led them to leave ANSYS to form Blue Ridge Numerics where they had *"a clean piece of paper, a start-up budget, and a lot of passion."*

Blue Ridge Numerics created a product that was very sophisticated, but where much of that sophistication was managed through default configurations for specific problems. This meant that hundreds of individual variables would be set automatically; allowing a design engineer to create something himself, without having to call in a CFD specialist. The second unique feature of their new software was that it operated on a PC, using the Windows operating system. Most of their competitors required a high-end workstation using the Unix operating system. At that time, such systems were priced ten times higher than comparable PCs, and were not generally available to design engineers. These two unique decisions placed a very powerful tool in the hands of people who could use it right at the beginning of the design of a new engine part or rocket nozzle. That product, CFDesign, helped to create an entirely new market for CFD software and placed Blue Ridge Numerics at its forefront. NASCAR Teams now have access to usable CFD to analyze the aerodynamics of their racecars and the performance of their engines.

CFDesign has a user interface that serves both novices and experts. Similar to the philosophy behind Microsoft Word, CFDesign has common default settings for its most powerful capabilities. This means that a novice can use it by manipulating only a few easily understood variables. However, there is considerable power available to an expert who has the necessary years of experience to manipulate all of the settings in the software. Most consumer software products now follow this approach. The software industry has recognized that customers use the application as its own learning environment, and do not have the luxury of being tutored in the tool by an outside expert. They have to be able to pick up the tool and start working. Williams and Schnipke broke with the accepted CFD industry practice of catering only to CFD experts.

Examining Blue Ridge's philosophy and behavior in serving customers, it is interesting to note, that they follow four of Tom Peter's top 12 behaviors of "insanely great companies". First, they have great talent. Schnipke is a veteran in the industry who has retained her grasp on the technical side of the business and, as CTO, represents the company's commitment to continue excelling in CFD technology through the best talent it can hire. The company is based in Charlottesville, Virginia, home of the University of Virginia, one of the leading research universities in the world. This is a city that is friendly to technology and business, and creates a comfortable and attractive home to retain its graduates.

Second, Blue Ridge Numerics was willing to "disrespect tradition." The CFD software industry had traditionally developed products that were strictly for experts in the field. They maintained that CFD could not be understood or used without a graduate degree in the field, and created software that focused on these very specialized people. This mind-set extended to decisions to deploy their software only on scientific workstations, and to avoid the more common PC Windows environment. Ed Williams and Rita Schnipke bucked this tradition and developed a software product specifically targeted at competent engineers that were still novices with CFD. They strove for a product that empowered these people to use CFD in the early design phases of a product. Bringing the tools down to the design engineers included deploying it on MS Windows.

Third, they were "totally passionate". They left executive positions in a larger company to pursue their vision of a new kind of fluid flow software. At the time, large industrial companies were decentralizing their engineering work. They had previously routed all CFD work to a central R&D organization. R&D would perform the analysis to the designers in the manufacturing branches. However, the turn around on this analysis could be as long as six months; reaching completion long after the product was already in production. Therefore, many companies were eager to find ways to place more responsibility into the hands of the manufacturing businesses and scale back their R&D groups.

This created an entirely new customer base for CFD software—a base that Blue Ridge Numerics was created specifically to address.

This drastic change in the customer base did not follow the "normal industry behavior" at all. Violation of such behavior is Tom Peter's fourth characteristic of success. Creating simplified software and deploying it on Windows PC's was the technical requirement, but a passionate belief that industry behavior should change was the final ingredient. Williams and Schnipke worked with companies to show them how to empower their design engineers to do their own CFD analysis, using Blue Ridge Numerics' CFDesign product.

Though argument and persuasive reasoning are one approach to this, it is much more effective to get a few successes under your belt, and let those show customers that there is a better way. A case study from Spalding Sporting Goods, illustrates the value of "Upfront CFD" (Blue Ridge's trademarked phrase for the process). Top-Flite, a leading brand of golf ball, was designed using Blue Ridge's CFDesign software and their Upfront CFD process. Spalding had traditionally used CFDesign to analyze the behavior of finished balls in flight; but they discovered that the software could also be used in the early design process to select the depth and size of the dimples on the ball, and to design-in specific behaviors. Deeper dimples caused the ball to fly lower in the air. Shallower dimples resulted in higher flight—up to a point. At some point, the dimples became too shallow to interact with the air efficiently. At this point, additional height comes at the cost of distance. Knowing this early in the process, allowed Spalding to experiment with dozens of unique designs for the golf ball; identifying the best pattern to put into production. But, it also built an internal knowledge base that many other companies do not possess. Not only does Spalding know which designs are best, they also know which designs are not good, and why they are not good. This knowledge has its own commercial value. They are now in a position to search out environments in which specialized types of performance are desired. This is very similar to the Post-it innovation, in which 3M scientists discovered glue that would not hold materials together permanently. Though not applicable to the main product lines, knowledge of this product allowed them to explore new products and create the extremely successful Post-it line.

Rita Schnipke spends a significant amount of time talking to customers, Blue Ridge's engineers, and engineers from across the industry. Her primary goal as CTO is to *"make sure that the technology is being driven toward the company's goal of being a design tool, and not being led off course by the whims of the individual developers."*

Executive

The executive pattern provides corporate or organizational leadership that touches on all aspects of the product or service provided. It is usually found in large companies, where the CTO works with the executive leaders on strategic directions, corporate vision, and the allocation of resources toward future capabilities.

Dawn Meyerriecks' role at DISA is an excellent example of this and was described in an earlier chapter.

Administrator

The administrator CTO is responsible for controlling budgets, identifying departmental synergies, and negotiations with vendors that provide information systems and technology-based products.

Washington State University's CTO and Vice President for Information Systems, Mary Doyle, finds herself focused on the strategic plan to deploy information technology throughout the organization. She is *"responsible for leading the policy, planning, development, deployment, operation, and maintenance of resources comprising the institution's core technology infrastructure."* This infrastructure includes campus networks, central administrative systems, university file and mail services, technology in university classrooms, the interactive television system for distance education, public broadcasting, and centrally provided technology support services. In concert with the President, Vice Presidents, Deans, and the University Advisory Committee for Computing and Telecommunications, Doyle plans and sets the direction for all matters involving information technology across the institution.

Dr. Doyle has also been appointed the Interim Director of Libraries at WSU. In this situation, the university recognizes that there is a fundamental relationship between IT and the libraries. *"Both units are in the information business and the coordination of this information infrastructure... is increasingly critical."* There are communities that argue that all libraries should and will become digital archives in the future. There are also those who argue that books and printed documents are historical artifacts in themselves; carrying much more value than just the information printed on the page. Doyle's strategic task is to identify the best ways to apply IT to library resources. She must satisfy the need for rapid and remote access to information that currently resides primarily on the printed page. But, she must also preserve the historical value of the rare and unique printed materials within the library's archives.

In the university environment, these types of policy decisions will require collaboration with the university President and multiple Deans. She must also deal with representatives from the state university system, state government, and student organizations advocating both sides of the issue.

"Our faculty, students, and staff, rely on technology for an increasing number of things they do every day, and the possibilities for the future are astounding. Advances in network technology, wireless technologies, advances in fiber optics and multi-media communications continue to change the way we work, study, and play," Doyle said. *"At the same time, we see an increased need for more serious attention to security, appropriate use, and copyright issues."*

Like the Department of Defense, libraries and universities are concerned about issues with security of data and systems, identity verification, and appropriate use of and access to information. As a CTO, Doyle can benefit from the significant investments that organizations like DISA are putting into these areas. Remaining abreast of the commercial availability of these technologies and the power that they possess, is a significant part of her administrative CTO role.

Advocate

The advocate pattern CTO represents the needs of the customer. This person often emerges from departments that were focused on the customer interface. Their perspective is not that of technology development, but more inclined toward the customer interface. Service organizations like Federal Express and government offices typically fall into this pattern.

Dr. Melody Mayberry-Stewart, Chief Technology Officer for the City of Cleveland, is responsible for developing, implementing, and supporting Information Technology (IT) strategies to improve government services for the City. Her challenge is to produce an IT-savvy government that uses the latest technology to be *"operational, efficient, and effective."*

A native Clevelander, Chief Mayberry-Stewart is the founder and CEO of the Black Diamond IT Consulting Group. She has more than 25 years of IT experience and works with CEOs, COOs, and CIOs to develop IT strategy and build high-performance IT organizations to improve organizational performance. She was the first African American female General Manager and Vice President of Corporate and Shared Services for worldwide delivery of IT systems and operations for the BP Amoco Corporation, where she had global responsibility for the design and implementation of IT systems and services. Prior to joining BP Amoco, Mayberry-Stewart was the first and only Black female Chief Information Officer (CIO) in the health care industry in the country. She was the CIO at Beth Israel Medical Center, with headquarters in New York City; earning more than $1 billion in revenues annually.

The City of Cleveland relies on Mayberry-Stewart to lead efforts to modernize its information infrastructure. The old infrastructure evolved as a number of disparate and incompatible systems. Through competitive contracting, the city has selected SBS Communications to design and deploy a new system that ties together all of the city services and makes them more accessible to the citizens.

Mayberry-Stewart inherited a city that had very poor technology penetration. Only 25% of city employees had access to email, governmental IT positions were staffed with minimally qualified individuals, and IT positions carried sub-standard pay levels; making it difficult to attract highly qualified candidates. She has been working with the city's Director of Finance to access the financial resources needed to fix this situation. However, she recognizes that technology systems must compete with other departments for the same limited pool of resources. They are constantly balancing purchases between new police cars, construction of new water processing plants, and upgrades to the IT infrastructure. She presents cities like Honolulu, Chicago, and Seattle as models for the capabilities she is targeting. One of her most important missions, is working with city council to educate them to the economic and social benefits of IT, and hopefully winning their support.

Case Western Reserve University has led the creation the OneCleveland organization to bring together non-profit and government agencies that can build a communications infrastructure within the city. Their goal is to promote education, training, cultural events, and access to government services for the population of Cleveland. This network will support the needs of schools, museums, hospitals, police and fire departments, and government offices to access high-speed networks for better internal operations and service to citizens. Through OneCleveland's efforts, each of these organizations will not have to build or purchase their own backbone infrastructure between their facilities, but will be able to leverage a common backbone supporting all city services. Mayberry-Stewart represents the interests of the City of Cleveland within this group, and provides expertise and insight into the needs of the city and the local government's plans to meet those needs.

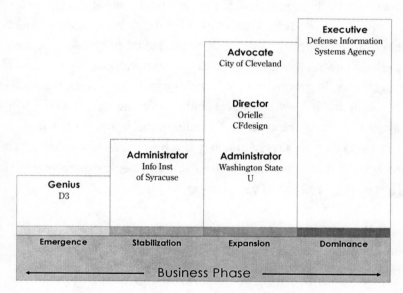

Figure 9.2 Matching the CTO to the Business Phase

Conclusion

This chapter explored the careers and responsibilities of several female CTOs. Throughout this research, we could find no differences between these women and their male counterparts. The women spanned all five of the major patterns of the CTO position, possessed similarly impressive backgrounds, and led successful organizations from start-ups to industry leaders. They emphasize the need to represent technology at the executive level of an organization. In business, technology decisions have a major impact on the company's ability to compete in the future. In government, it provides significant advantages on the battlefield and in services to local citizens. In the public sector, technology has a strong impact on the educational opportunities that are available in a university. Technology has become an important part of most products and services. Therefore, the strategic management of it is a core part of a company's success.

10

DEFENSE CTO

This paper presents five major activities through which the CTO of a defense contractor can contribute to the success and competitive position of the company. Through active involvement in the architecture of company products, research partnerships, new business development, program reviews, and competitive evaluations, the CTO can have a significant impact on the ability of the company to both win new government contracts, and to succeed on existing contracts. The technical expertise, corporate-wide relationships, and influence of the CTO, are essential ingredients within a defense contracting company, and must be applied toward the strategic goals of the company; not just on a few selected projects.

System Architecture	Research Partnerships	Business Development	Program Reviews	Competitive Evaluation
• Engineering • New Technology • Design Processes	• Corp Relationships • Industry Leaders • Technology Leaders	• Marketing • Customer Needs	• Operations • Management	• Corporate • Strategy

The position of the Chief Technology Officer is unique in most businesses, but most writers and practitioners agree that the CTO must make corporate-wide contributions to the company's competitive position. Within the computer industry, this may mean focusing on the perfect architecture of the hardware design, as championed by Greg Papadopoulos at Sun Microsystems.

> *"The greatest CTOs that I know are the ones that take architecture seriously. Architecture guides the constraints and shows what's important and what isn't. It bridges the creativity of the engineer to something that can achieve a high impact for the company."*
> (Baldwin, 2004)

David Whelan, of Boeing Space and Communications, has a defense-modified perspective of this responsibility that is quite complementary to Papadopoulos[7].

> *"The CTO nurtures and cultivates new ideas and innovation in both the technologies and the processes by which we build and design large complex aerospace systems. The CTO must focus the enterprise or company so it can be responsive to new technology and capitalize on it."* (Aspatore, 2000)

Both of these CTOs are in the manufacturing business; one for commercial products, and the other for defense systems. But both of them recognize that the CTO's actions must have a strategic impact on the position of the company. William Lewis described this responsibility in his paper in the Sloan Management Review.

> *"The CTO's key tasks are not those of lab director writ large but, rather, of a technical business person deeply involved in shaping and implementing overall corporate strategy."* (Lewis, 1990)

In this paper, we will discuss several ways in which a CTO has the opportunity to make contributions to the strategic position of a defense contracting company. Some of these contributions are common to other industries; others are unique to the defense industrial environment.

System Architecture

Greg Papadopoulos, at Sun Microsystems, is focused on the architecture of computer workstations and other systems that his company is building. He recognizes that the overall system architecture dictates performance limitations on the computer, and has a huge influence on its scalability, flexibility, and reliability. In his view, the CTO can make the greatest contribution to the company by focusing his attention on this aspect, and insuring that years of experience and education are used to optimize the architecture of new products.

It is not sufficient for a technology leader like a CTO to listen to the market and build the capabilities they are asking for. Papadopoulos explains it this way, *"Extrapolation in this business is really dangerous. If you sort of take what the market is asking for right now and what people think they need, that's what I should be investing in. That gets you into some serious trouble in computing. You sort of follow the conventional wisdom, and you sort of end up three years from now having built the thing that people wanted three years before."* (Papadopoulos, 2003)

The CTO is not told what to build by a demanding market. Instead, technology leaders must divine the future needs of the market, before the demand exists, and build to that vision. Missing the mark can cost millions of dollars and the competitive position of the company. It is essential that a CTO, and others supporting him, have a reliable vision of the future or the ability to extrapolate a number of current trends, advances, and needs toward their future convergence in a product.

David Whelan, of Boeing, echoes Papadopoulos' perspective for defense systems. He recognizes that innovation and new ideas are going to strongly influence the company's ability to win major government contracts and to perform on them as promised. Large companies and large customers can be drawn into the trap of merely renovating old solutions, rather than creating radical new solutions that can deliver a 100X performance improvement. Defense CTOs push the company and the customer out of their comfort zone and toward embracing next-generation concepts and technologies. A defense company can win a number of contracts based on a single, unique innovation. But the string of wins is limited by the time it takes the competition to replicate that innovation or create one better. Therefore, the CTO is not charged with pattern-breaking innovation on every project, but must set an aggressive pace to keep company innovation ahead of the competition.

The classic defense technology example of this is stealth technology. The engineers working under Kelly Johnson at Lockheed's Skunk Works facility in Palmdale, California, began with the mission of building a high-flying spy plane; the U-2. But, the Soviet Union's eventual ability to intercept the U-2 at 70,000 feet, led to the demand for new planes with speed, altitude, and stealth. The Skunks Works imbued the SR-71 with basic stealth materials and a low radar cross-section. As materials, manufacturing, and computer technologies improved, they were able to create even more advanced designs that resulted in the F-117 Stealth Fighter (Rich & Janos, 1996). Plunging into the new field of stealth, gave Lockheed a head start and an advantage over every other defense contractor. They were able to maintain this advantage through several generations of aircraft. Stealth is a key technology that can be applied to a number of different aircraft, and even seacraft. One innovation can be applied to a number of products, but scientists must continue to push the technology forward, because if they don't, the eager geniuses at the competitors will do so. Eventually, Northrop joined the elite ranks of stealth aircraft manufacturers and challenged Lockheed in the field that it had dominated. This competition continues today, though at classified levels that are not accessible for business analysis.

William Lewis further pushes Whelan's image of the CTO as a strategic part of the corporation. He or she should not be relegated to a single system such as a single new rocket, aircraft, or combat vehicle, but should be involved in shaping the corporate strategy that will position the company to win multiple major product contracts.

As an example of technical positioning for multiple contracts, we examine the development of new IT and electronics architectures for military training ranges. These ranges have evolved over a number of decades to support every form of electronic communication between ground and air vehicles, command posts, control centers, and computer laboratories. The software and communication infrastructure for every system on the range is unique, and requires its own team of maintenance personnel and programmers. As new systems are added or existing systems are improved, corresponding but unique changes are made to every system on the range. As the number of such systems has grown from a hand-full to dozens, this maintenance task has become extremely expensive and prone to multiple errors. These software and communications systems can become extremely fragile and on the verge of breakdown at any time.

Recognizing that multiple customers are faced with this situation, a CTO may champion a standard architecture for the next generation of systems procured to replace all of these legacy systems. The architecture defines interfaces, infrastructures, standard tools, and a complete system design for all equipment operating on the range. It is a roadmap or blueprint that enforces standardization, reuse, and complementary functionality across the entire training range. Such a standard architecture is designed to become the foundation for winning multiple contracts, and establishing the company as the leader in solving complex systems integration problems. This is Papadopoulos' architecture-centric focus of the CTO. In this case, the architecture is not that of a computer system, but of an entire network of computers, electronics equipment, and communication systems. It encompasses the hardware and software of the systems, but also the processes for designing and building the system, and the education required to maintain it. This is a complete lifecycle solution to the problem.

IBM Fellow, Grady Booch, is applying this same approach to complex software systems, though he refers to it as championing, identifying, cataloging, and applying software patterns. He is single-mindedly focused on using these patterns to escape from reinventing old software and repeating old errors, to building larger and more complex systems on a foundation or architecture of reliable patterns that do not have to be reinvented for every new project (Scannell, 2004).

Research Partnerships

Within defense companies, pure research along the lines of the IBM T.J. Watson Research Center, GE Research Labs, or the old Bell Labs is rare. There are some specialty companies that pursue only research-oriented contracts like those offered by the Defense Advanced Research Projects Agency (DARPA). These companies and DARPA create prototypes than can be fielded on a one-off basis, or that can serve as the catalyst for a new system. Large developers such Lockheed Martin, Northrop Grumman, and Boeing, do not survive on such projects, but they do pursue them as a source of innovation for larger projects. Small research projects may lead to new materials for stealth aircraft, new forms of sensors, computers designed for cognitive processing, or software capable of mining all federal databases. Each can contribute a valuable advantage to the bid for a major military system that can sustain the company for a decade.

Most government offices and many large programs also have their own internal research budgets. This money can pay for a number of new technologies that the CTO can mine for application across a business unit or the entire company. Left untapped, the technology may find itself limited to a single program or remain completely untapped. Unfortunately, when research is funded separate from an active program, it is all too easy for the results to languish in final reports and briefings while the innovators move on to the next exciting research project. Without a technology mining team to capture and distribute the results, the research investment is lost or under leveraged.

Valuable research can also be mined from DoD and university labs. The Naval, Air Force, and Army Research Laboratories conduct some very important investigations targeted directly at the problems that their service branches are facing right now. These labs are usually willing, or even eager, to share their results with companies that are building combat systems for the DoD. The CTO must insure that relevant projects in these laboratories are being tapped. Universities conduct this same kind of research under government funding, and often welcome industrial partnerships.

In support of this model, Henry Chesbrough maintains that modern challenges and business limitations demand that partnerships with external research organizations are essential. No one company can attract and retain all of the expertise necessary to meet their future needs. Chesbrough's open innovation attempts to leverage the capabilities of corporate, university, and government labs toward a common goal (Chesbrough, 2003). This allows each to achieve more than they could alone; and more importantly, to achieve more than a competitor who will not practice open innovation. These ideas are the natural next step in the industrial arms race to remain ahead of the competition. The CTO will play a pivotal role in investigating potential partners, recommending relationships, and negotiating terms that allow the company to profit from the partnerships. Choosing the wrong partners or allowing them to reap the lion's share of the profits will be devastating to the company.

New Business Development

The lifeblood of a defense contractor is the winning of new government contracts. These are extremely competitive bids for everything from new combat aircraft to lawn maintenance on a foreign base. In each case, the company must present a solution that best meets the customers' needs and does so at a competitive price. Unlike the retail industry, companies cannot afford to develop multiple versions of a product and hope that enough customers purchase one to justify the investment. For many combat systems, there is exactly one customer, and that customer will purchase every system through a single contract. Therefore, the CTO must make his or her technological contribution in the proposal or prototype phase of the project.

In this case, the CTO may not be the actual writer serving on the proposal team, but will contribute by ensuring that relevant technical talent is available to create the technology side of a winning solution. Small contracts usually attract the existing staff that works on similar projects. They represent the level of practice of the company, but not necessarily the highest level of expertise that the company has in that field. The CTO can contribute to major proposals by tapping into the resources of the entire company, and bringing experts to bear who are not necessarily working a legacy project day-to-day. The CTO may be able to bring in scientists and managers from research labs and to tap into the partnerships that the company has with outside organizations. These contributions become more important as the contract under pursuit becomes larger, and represents the heart of the company's business area; the so-called "must win" projects.

The CTO must apply the technical capabilities of the company toward these proposals, since this is the source of all revenue for the company. It is not acceptable for a CTO to apply the company's technology only after a contract is won, and design and production are underway.

Inserting innovation into a proposal requires that the people doing so are aware of the latest changes to the military's strategy and mission. For example, the recent "Transformation" of the military has a direct impact on the capabilities of all of the systems that they are purchasing. New systems cannot just improve the capabilities of their predecessors, but must be designed to carry out entirely new missions. Companies that understand this are positioned to grow, and companies that do not understand the new mission are positioned to shrink and be acquired. As an example, the recent issue of Transformation Trends published by the DoD Office of Force Transformation called for new approaches to deploying our forces to trouble spots around the world. Traditionally reliant upon naval vessels to move large volumes of material, the article points toward the potential power of Ultra-Large Airlifters, a.k.a. dirigibles (DoD, 2004). Too many these images are part of the past; something used in World War II and seldom seen since the Hindenberg disaster. However, the transformation of the military is calling upon these airlifters to carry much heavier loads than can be handled by aircraft, and to move faster than naval ships. Understanding these trends, why they exist, and who is pushing them, is an essential part of positioning a defense company for future success and winning major contracts. The CTO must insure that the company has the technical expertise to compete in these new domains.

Program Review

Another opportunity for CTO contribution to the company is in the review of major programs. Typically, the level of expertise available to each program is limited or uneven. It is the result of historical accumulation of staff ad expertise, directed hiring success, and the outflow of expertise. The staff may have extensive expertise in a field like materials fabrication, but be very unskilled in a field like software deployment; though both are essential to the success of the project. The CTO should be prepared to suggest external sources of expertise or the necessity for hiring the skills that are missing.

As an example, following the anthrax release at the Brentwood Post Office in Washington, DC, one defense company CTO recognized the opportunity to apply the company's medical sterilization technology to the sterilization of mail. He worked with the government to ensure that the contract was awarded and the system successfully installed. Following installation he continued to participate in the operation of the system and identified a number of improvements to the system to reduce the negative impacts of sterilization. Since this was a very new application, there were no validated guidelines for the process and an in-depth, scientific understanding of the technology was required to determine when the Anthrax spores had been killed. In this case, the expertise of the CTO was in the electron beam technology being used for sterilization (McKnight, 2002).

Defense projects require sophisticated project management skills, but they must also require expert-level technical oversight. In most cases, the CTO him/herself will not be able to provide that expertise directly. But, just as essential, as a reviewer, the CTO will be in a position to recognize opportunities for technological improvements and will have the authority to access expertise across the company.

Peter Bridenbaugh, former CTO at ALCOA, provided this oversight when steel production mini-mills first began to emerge. He recognized the significance of technical advancements that made it possible for mini-mills to operate profitably and to assault the markets held by large metal producing companies like Alcoa. Because he was actively monitoring new technologies and assessing their applicability to business opportunities, Bridenbaugh was in a position to advise Alcoa of this threat while mini-mills still occupied a very limited niche in metals production. Other executives within Alcoa had come up through the operational and scientific ranks, but because they were no longer intimately familiar with the latest scientific developments in metal production, the emergence of mini-mills did not appear to be a serious threat to Alcoa's business. Bridenbaugh's involvement allowed ALCOA to prepare for the competition and make early decisions about whether to defend this niche or move into other areas (Smith, 2003). Clayton Christensen warns that this type of disruptive innovation from the outside is one of the major threats to a business (Christensen & Raynor, 2004). Within the defense industry, these threats are constantly emerging for business areas that have low barriers to entry, or when government policy dictates some form of revenue/contract sharing among competitors or with small businesses.

Competitive Evaluation

If the CTO is involved in program reviews, system architecture decisions, research commercialization, and new business development, then he should be very well versed in the position of the company within the industry. This understanding is valuable for identifying the company's current competitive position and targeting changes that are necessary to maintain or improve that position.

Every company has a capabilities profile that defines its position in the industry. That profile and their current position have a very strong influence on future prospects. Projections of the future needs of the Department of Defense are useful for identifying the type of technical expertise that the company will need to win future DoD contracts. The CTO must participate in corporate-wide evaluations of their position and preparations for the future. The CTO may also initiate technology-specific evaluations to complement the larger activities of the CEO, COO, and others in the executive ranks.

These evaluations may uncover areas in which the company needs to change their hiring or education policies in order to cultivate the necessary skills within the company. They may also indicate shortcomings that are too large to compensate for internally. In this case, a strategic acquisition or partnership may be called for. The CTO's team may need to scour a specific field for a company that can fit well within their own organization, or that is motivated to build a complimentary teaming relationship. The goal is to create a company or partnership that is more powerful than the competitor—and to do so early enough for that power to be applied effectively when a major competition begins.

Conclusion

If the CTO is to be a true executive level position, then it must be focused on the strategic activities and decisions of the business. The CTO is not a project-specific resource that is expected to apply his or her own expertise in one field. Instead, the CTO should be able to move beyond their own expertise to understand the technical capital residing within the company, and to identify opportunities to apply it effectively. In this article, we have sometimes described the CTO's contributions as those of a single individual. However, the CTO is, in fact, more a catalyst for an entire team of people, and to some degree, an entire company. For a company of any significant size, it is impossible for one individual to assimilate a complete understanding of the company's abilities or participate in all of the important activities prescribed above. This is a job for members of the CTO staff. Just as the CIO heads a staff of IT personnel and provides strategic guidance to their actions, the CTO office will rely upon the expertise of a permanent and ad hoc staff to perform these functions.

11

CTO RELATIONSHIPS

The CTO position was initially created to ensure that senior management paid appropriate attention to their corporate technological capabilities (Betz, 1993). Attracting this attention and operating as an effective member of the executive team, requires that the CTO nurture relationships with a number of people and groups internal and external to the company.

Chief Executive Officer and Executive Committees

Providing strategic advice to the CEO and the Executive Committee requires much more than technical expertise. The CTO must earn the trust and confidence of the CEO. In previous positions, the CTO may have earned the respect and confidence of peers and superiors through technical prowess and performance. But, this new position requires business prowess and financial performance (Larson, 2001). The CTO must exhibit a clear understanding of, and dedication to, improving the competitive position of the company.

The acceptance of the CTO as a business strategist is an important step. It will determine whether the CTO is treated as an equal member of the executive team, or is isolated as an outside source for technical advice and information. Ed Roberts' study of the strategic management of technology indicates that most companies include the CTO on the Executive Committee along with the CEO, COO, CFO, and CIO. In North America, 60% of the companies surveyed included the CTO on this committee. In Europe, the number was 67% and in Japan it was 91% (Roberts, 2001). In some companies, the CTO actually teaches senior management about the importance of technology in their industry. The goal is to ingrain technology as a significant consideration in all executive decision-making (Gwynne, 1996; Earl & Feeney, 2000).

CTOs are not the first officers to face the challenge of inclusion or exclusion from the strategic process. When the CIO position emerged, they too were branded as technologists who could not function as business strategists (Kwak, 2001). This image has diminished as CIOs have shown themselves to be just as effective at making business decisions as their management-schooled peers. Kwak cites the results of a study of pairs of executives at 69 companies that indicated that the business acumen of CIOs was equal to that of their executive peers. Another study of 417 construction company executives, found that eighty percent of the CIOs in those companies were considered equal contributors of the strategic decision making process (Phair & Rubin, 1998). Therefore, the CTO should be able to learn from the integration experience of the CIO. Executive Committee members should also recognize that the technological stereotype that was not accurate for the CIO might also prove to be inaccurate for the CTO.

If the CTO is to provide business decisions and advice, there needs to be some measure of the quality of this advice. The CTOs performance should be measured against a plan worked out with the CEO. This plan may include achieving milestones, introducing new products, reducing costs, reducing uncertainty, and selecting the right research projects to fund. Bill Waite advocates a customized set of metrics for the CTO. Within his company, these included maintaining and teaching technology within the organization, measuring the speed at which technology is brought into the organization, the rate at which the CTO turns technology into salable intellectual property, and the CTO's effectiveness as the custodian for research and development money.

Chief Information Officer

Many organizations have a difficult time separating the responsibilities of the CTO from those of the CIO, which can make the working relationship between the two very difficult. At the 2001 InfoWorld CTO Forum, CTOs from Sun Microsystems, eBay, Dell Computer, and other companies, identified their responsibilities as being externally focused while the CIO's responsibilities were internally focused (Spiers, 2001). Corporations have realized that they need a CIO to oversee the application of technology to internal operations. This has included computer systems for accounting, billing, telephony, security, and a host of other functions. Prior to the creation of the CTO position, the CIO was the only executive technologist, and was often called upon to support manufacturing computerization, the purchase of computer aided design packages, and strategic decisions for injecting technology into products (Kwak, 2001).

The internal/external division of responsibilities is a very useful differentiation, but it leaves significant gray areas that can result in turf wars between the two players. Therefore, the CTO's relationship with the CIO should be based on a more clearly defined division of responsibility. The goal is to create a complementary and supportive relationship that maximizes contributions to corporate strategy and profitability.

Chief Scientist

Chief Scientists are much more intimately involved in the day-to-day execution of scientific and technical projects. Each of these is usually limited to the laboratory, division, or facility in which he or she resides. As described earlier, senior technologists are often very eager to explore new areas. But, these explorations should be harnessed to contribute to the company's strategic direction. Earl maintained that a company should not have a separate technology strategy. Supporting this perspective, one study has found that short-term, product focused R&D is positively correlated with the financial performance of the company, while long-term R&D is negatively correlated with it (Roberts, 2001). That is one reason that it is important for the CTO to mentor the Chief Scientists, and to direct their focus such that it contributes to the success of the company.

Chief Scientists may also have informal networks of technologists that span business areas, but they do not have the official charter to cross-pollinate technologies. The CTO can organize an internal council of technologists to search out and apply the best technologies available across the company (Brunner, 2001). Darren McKnight of Titan, reports that he sponsored internal summits to bring leading technologists together to share ideas. He viewed it as his responsibility to create leverage across many different business groups to identify potential combinations of technology that could become new products or services. He is currently working on plans to create a network of technologists similar to that described by Brunner (McKnight, 2002).

CMGI was one of the leading incubators of the Internet business explosion. Daniel Jaye, the CTO of Engage, a CMGI incubated company, felt that the cross-pollination of technologies within CMGI could identify valuable opportunities and solve local problems. Therefore, acting as the ad hoc CTO of the parent company, he organized technology summits for all CMGI technology leaders. One of these summits led to the realization that two CMGI companies were buying services from the same vendor. The leaders reasoned that the vendor would be a good fit under the CMGI umbrella and purchased the company, reducing outsourcing costs and adding a proven product to the CMGI family (Aspatore, 2000).

Table 2. Key Roles and Responsibilities of Technical Leaders

CTO	*Technology Strategy.* The CTO's primary responsibility is contributing to the strategic direction of the company by identifying the role that specific technologies will play in its future growth. The CTO looks for contributions that technology can make to the competitive advantage of the company.
	Internal Coordination. Identification of the best technologies usually comes from a strong internal network of people who are in touch with the latest technologies and understand their potential.
	External Partnerships. Like all business professionals, the CTO will be part of a strong network that includes business partners, academics, government officials, and technology thought leaders.
CIO	*Information Technology Application.* The CIO leads the application of information technology to internal processes and services. This person is responsible for improving the efficiency of internal systems such as payroll, accounting, accounts receivable, labor recording, benefits management, human resources records, government reporting, and a number of others.
	Reduce Internal Operating Costs. The CIO's systems are focused on reducing the costs associated with the company operations listed above.
	Improve Services to Employees and Partners. CIOs and IT departments have provided fantastic improvements in employee services in the last two decades. They have also built systems that allow better information and financial exchange with business partners.

Chief Scientist	*Technology Creation.* Chief Scientists lead teams that are focused on creating new technologies. Given strategic direction from management, these teams work to create products or services that make the company's strategy possible and that do so in a manner superior to their competitors.
	Recognized Leader. Chief Scientists should be recognized leaders in their technical field. They should be actively involved in professional associations and conferences with their peers in industry and academia.

Research and Development Laboratories

Since the 1960s, research and development laboratories have been transformed from independent scientists working on challenging, but questionably marketable technologies, to organizations that are expected to make direct contributions to company profits. The CTO can play an important role in monitoring and directing these labs. Erickson *et al* (1990) recommend several principles that a CTO should use for directing R&D. First, R&D personnel should be kept in touch with the company's customers and markets. Few labs can seclude themselves from the market and conduct research for its own sake. Second, the CTO should foster open communications between R&D staff, manufacturing engineers, and the marketing department. Third, the CTO should hold the R&D labs to schedule and budget commitments. If an R&D project is not delivering results, it may need to be terminated and the funds applied more productively elsewhere. Some long-standing projects constantly show great promise and absorb resources, but produce nothing. These projects, though considered "pillars of the lab," must be held accountable and face termination if they do not produce results (Earl & Feeny, 1994).

R&D laboratory budgets should be the topic of critical reviews by the executive staff. The CTO should lead initial funding reviews in which R&D projects present the expectations for the project, its applicability to market needs, the position relative to competitors, and a record of past successes. The CTO should also hold in-progress reviews to monitor problems and successes. A CTO can serve as an honest broker in these reviews, because he or she comes from outside of the laboratory and is not personally involved in the projects (Robb, 1994; Media Lab, 2001).

Sales and Marketing

CTOs, like Rajeev Bharadwaj at Ejasent and Ron Moritz at Symantec, are actively involved in marketing products and services. These CTOs recognize that some products are so technically sophisticated, that explaining them to the trade media requires a technical representative. When the CTO is used to explain the subtle, but significant, differences between the company's products and those of competitors, he or she becomes a de facto member of the marketing staff (Foster, 2000).

Working with the sales and marketing departments also insures that the CTO remains rooted in the customers' need for the product, rather than the technical sophistication of the product. Supporting this perspective, Michael Wolfe of Kana Communications, says that, *"Creating a product is mapping what a customer needs to what you can build"* (Aspatore, 2000). Making this mapping requires regular and detailed interactions with customers and the marketplace.

Technology and Executive Leadership

Companies began adding Chief Technology Officers to the executive ranks in the 1980s, because technology was becoming an integral part of many strategic decisions and future plans. The CIO already provided strong expertise on the internal application of technology. But, senior managers needed expert advice regarding the inclusion of technologies in existing products and the creation of new products and services with large technical components. A CTO that is actively involved in monitoring new technologies, separating marketing rhetoric from technical facts, and identifying profitable applications for those technologies, can make a significant difference in the company's competitive future. The CTO can also add value to the company by participating in government, academic, and industry groups in a manner that creates positive attention for the company.

Technology companies are involved in thousands of acquisitions every year. Selecting the best target for an acquisition often requires reliable advice on technical issues at the executive level. The CTO is also a valuable tool in addressing the increasingly well-informed media about the products, services, and the future plans of the company. CTOs can speak as peers to other technologists, and can play a role in convincing the media that the company's decisions are sound and will add value for the company's stakeholders.

It is important that the CTO not become the senior technologist of the company. Instead, he or she is the senior business executive with a focus on technology. In the CTO position, senior management is not looking for enthusiastic advice from a research scientist. Instead, they need sound advice on business decisions involving technology.

12

THE EVOLUTION OF INNOVATION

n 1856, William Henry Perkin was an 18 year-old student at Britain's Royal College of Chemistry. He was working toward an antimalarial drug that was important to the British Empire as it expanded into Africa. But, he stumbled onto a coal-tar derivative that was particularly effective at staining silk material into a rich shade of purple. At a time when dull, earthen colors had dominated clothing for two centuries, Perkin realized that a vibrant and stable purple dye was a very valuable product. He quit the university against the protests of his professors, and established a factory for producing the dye. His father invested the family's entire fortune in the endeavor and his brother quit a job in the building trades to manage the new business. By 1857, Perkin's factory was producing "Tyrian Purple" for sale to commercial silk dyers, and he was working on new dyes for wool and cotton (Buderi, 2000).

The success of Tyrian Purple as a commercial venture, led chemists across Europe to focus on this market, in the hope of making their own fortunes. Over the next fifty years, major companies like Bayer, Hochst, BASF, and AGFA built their fortunes through the creation of new dyes. The sustained demand for dyes built new factories, created a demand for educated chemists, raised the importance of a university education, and provided employment for thousands of workers. The plot of this 19th century story closely matches that of current Silicon Valley computer, software, and web services companies—the curiosity, hard work, and good luck of one person leads to the creation of one unique product; followed by the invigoration of an industry.

Formal Study of Innovation Is New

The creation of the aniline purple dye was an invention. The application of that dye as a commercial product was an innovation. Both invention and innovation are very old processes. The history of weaponry, machinery, and transportation are all filled with instances of invention and innovation that transformed individuals, companies, countries, and economies. But, as old as these practices are, the formal study of innovation is relatively new; tracing it roots back to the works of Burns and Stalker in 1961, and Rogers in 1962. In *The Management of Innovation*, Burns and Stalker clearly separated mechanistic from organic environments. In a mechanistic environment, it is best to create standard processes, rules, and hierarchy to improve the efficiency of the organization. But, organic environments require a different approach; one which recognizes the importance of unique skills and knowledge, as well as the means to stimulate these toward solving new problems and creating new products. Organic working environments require employees to use their own knowledge and judgment to solve a continually changing set of problems. In *Diffusion of Innovation*, Rogers investigated the means by which new ideas propagate through a society. He was most interested in the social factors that allowed ideas to prosper and identified five variables that determine the rate of adoption of a new idea or product; the attributes of the innovation itself, the type of decision required to adopt an innovation, the communication channels through which the idea is carried, the nature of the social system into which the idea is introduced, and the extent of a specific change agent's promotional efforts. These ideas, published 45 years ago, were some of the first models of innovation.

It could also be argued that the ideas of Fredrick Winslow Taylor in 1911, and Joseph Schumpeter in 1942, were about innovation. Taylor may have invented new shapes and sizes of shovels to implement his ideas about labor productivity, but the real innovation was in recognizing that traditional methods of factory work were inefficient and could be improved if a scientific mind were allowed to enforce practices on the working hands of laborers. This idea so threatened the positions of laborers, that Taylor found himself defending it in court and before Congress. The immediate affront to labor was much clearer to most people than the long-term economic benefits of efficiency, profitability, and lower costs. Schumpeter and David Wells (Perelman, 1995) pointed out that inefficiencies in business cannot be sustained indefinitely. New ideas and new technology will transform a single practice or an entire industry to eliminate these inefficiencies. Schumpeter's "creative destruction" is the march of invention, innovation, and change across the face of society and business. Though it is painful to many people, it accrues to the good of the entire society. Individual interests cannot stop this march, but they can rush to get in front of it, so that they are on the creative side of change; not just its destructive side.

> Could the invention of the methods of innovation be the greatest invention of the 20th century?

Transient Value of Innovation

Today, we describe innovation as an activity or action that creates value from materials, processes, or ideas that are available to many people, but which have not been recognized or applied by others. But, like Perkin's discovery of purple dye, the success of an innovation will draw others seeking to capitalize on similar ideas or seeking to copy them outright. This value is a very transient thing that, unprotected, will flow from an inventor to a competitor without regard to claims of ownership. In fact, the entire system of patents, copyrights, and legal IP protection, exists to allow inventors and innovators to prosper from their work. We recognize the value of innovation to society, the economy, and business, and are eager to foster the personal and organizational investments that are required to make it happen. However, the time limits on these legal protections must also balance the good of the creator with the good of society. Legal systems allow a temporary monopoly as a means of encouraging and rewarding innovation, but prevent long-term control of an idea that can benefit an entire society.

Once the value of innovation was both recognized and protected, it became desirable to analyze the practice and attempt to formalize it for repeatability. Establishing a business on a single innovation is a great entrepreneurial venture; but sustaining an ongoing business through random and haphazard innovation is much too risky. I suggest that our understanding of innovation has also evolved so that it can be practiced in a disciplined, organized, and directed manner; or one can continue to pursue it in a random and haphazard way (Figure 12.1).

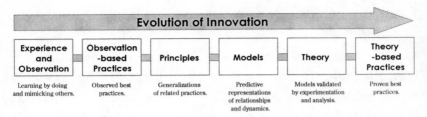

Experience and Observation	Observation-based Practices	Principles	Models	Theory	Theory-based Practices
Learning by doing and mimicking others.	Observed best practices.	Generalizations of related practices.	Predictive representations of relationships and dynamics.	Models validated by experimentation and analysis.	Proven best practices.

Figure 12.1 Innovation has evolved from individual experiences and observations to practices based on theories.

How Innovation Evolves

In its native form, innovation begins with *observation and experience.* Someone notices something valuable and repeats the activity to repeat the benefits. This may come from a new technology, a new process, or a unique application of something that has been around for years.

These observations lead to *practices* that appear to capture the value noticed in observation. The practice-stage of innovation focuses on selecting and fine-tuning specific practices to improve results. However, practices are very limited and not immediately extensible to other businesses, activities, or products. Therefore, practices are soon extended into principles.

Principles are rules that seem to generalize the important aspects of specific practices. The foundational literature of management, the works of Henri Fayol and Chester Barnard, focused on extracting general principles from their years of experiences, observations, and practices. They hoped to provide a foundation upon which big businesses could be built and thrive; without reliance on the intuition and experience of a single outstanding leader.

Where principles derive from historical information, *models* attempt to structure this knowledge so that it can be extrapolated to future applications. Models attempt to describe both facts and the relationships between them to create a dynamic representation that can identify what the past and present mean to the future. Most models do not claim to be exact representations of a real system, but rather capture useful information and make predictions better than a less structured view of that information.

Innovation *theories* attempt to get at an absolute truth about a system. They separate legend, intuition, precedent, and varied practices from objective truths that can be counted upon to deliver exact results. Theories are based on experimentation and analysis. Because of their exactness, the breadth of theories may be limited by what can actually be proven. But theories also serve as a solid foundation upon which new ideas and experiments can be built.

Finally, *theory-based practices* close the loop. These replace limited observations with limited theories in describing the most appropriate practices. Theory-based practice is the core foundation of science. But in management, the entire spectrum of innovation from Figure 1 is at work daily across the world economy.

Moving to Theory-based Practice

Historically, practicing businesses have worked from observation, experience, practices, and principles, while models and theories have been the realm of academics, researchers, and consultants. Combining these two communities allows practitioners to move from observation-based practices to theory-based practices. Since this progression of understanding takes time, it assumes that the derived theories remain applicable to the environment from which the data was collected. In a fast changing field, it may be impossible to create theories at a pace that remains current with the environment in which it will be applied. In some fields, change is so rapid that practices based in observation are better than those based on theory, because of the currency of observations and the age of the information upon which a theory is built.

The sheer number of popular books on innovation indicates that most practices and models are based on observations rather than theories. A search of the Amazon.com database identifies 12,560 available titles on "innovation". When the search is narrowed to business titles published in the last 20 years, the list shrinks to 2,371. Figure 12.2 shows how these titles are distributed over each year, clearly indicating a rapid increase in 1997—the year that Clayton Christensen's *Innovator's Dilemma* appeared.

Innovation Books Published Annually

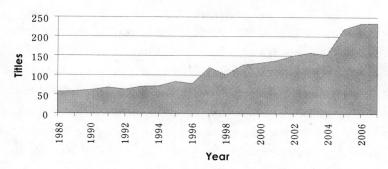

Figure 12.2 Annual book titles on the topic of innovation has risen from 56 titles in 1988 to 235 titles in 2007, resulting in a cumulative twenty year library of 2,371 titles.
Source: Amazon.com

Buderi's account of 19th century Bayer identifies one of the company founders as a chemist. The company showed its persistence in creating new products using every means possible. It initially tried to create new products on the manufacturing floor as an integrated part of the production process. When this failed, they experimented with hiring chemists and allowing them to remain at their universities to interact with other faculty members; seeking to isolate their chemists from the distractions of production problems. This did not yield results within one year, so the company pulled the chemists back to the factories and assigned them to specific production lines. However, Carl Duisberg, one of the young chemists, settled into a research lab and spent the next two years inventing three new colors for the company. Bayer's persistence in trying new methods along with the arrival of a talented researcher led to new products, higher profits, and a much larger research organization, focused on Duisberg; who later became a member of the company's board of directors.

The Innovation Imperative

Regarding invention, innovation, change, and renewal, Charles Kettering told the United States Chamber of Commerce in 1929, *"I am not pleading with you to make changes. I am telling you; you have got to make them—not because I say so, but because old Father Time will take care of you if you don't change. Advancing waves of other people's progress sweep over the unchanging man and wash him out. Consequently, you need to organize a department of systematic change-making."* (Buderi, 2000)

Alfred North Whitehead famously said that, *"The greatest invention of the nineteenth century was the invention of the method of invention"* (Whitehead, 1925). What has been the greatest invention of the twentieth century and how are we using it in the twenty-first century? Could it be the invention of the methods of innovation? What do we really understand about innovation? That will be the primary focus of this column. We will explore current principles, models, and theories of innovation and make some attempt to understand how best to use them.

Definitions

Innovation:

- the introduction of something new (Merriam-Webster On-line)
- an idea, practice, or object that is perceived as new by an individual or other unit of adoption (Rogers, 1962)
- an activity or action that creates value from materials, processes, or ideas that are available to many people, but which have not been recognized or explored by others

Model:

- to abstract from reality a description of a dynamic system (Fishwick, 1995)
- a representation of an actual system (Banks, 1998)

13

UNDERSTANDING AND ACQUIRING TECHNOLOGY ASSETS FOR GLOBAL COMPETITION

Technology has become an integral part of nearly every business and social endeavor. However, in spite of this, each profession has different definitions for what technology is. A universally shared definition has not emerged—which indicates that the transformation of these professions by technology is still occurring faster than it can be codified.

A physical scientist might describe technology as the set of equipment and apparatus that are used for scientific experiments. A social scientist would make a more vague reference to the underlying change agent that is advancing society. An IT professional sees technology as the computer hardware and software that is used to automate internal business operations. A manufacturing plant manager might suggest that technology refers to all of the assets that enable and enhance production operations. An economist sees technology as an enabling force in society that can make significant improvements to productivity, on a global scale. The diversity of these perspectives is an indication of the pervasiveness of technology, and the challenges associated with understanding how it impacts business and social activities.

Burgelman, Christensen, and Wheelwright (2004) define technology as,

> "...the theoretical and practical knowledge, skills, and artifacts that can be used to develop products and services, as well as their production and delivery systems. Technologies can be embodied in people, materials, cognitive and physical processes, plants, equipment, and tools. Key elements of technology may be implicit; existing only in an embedded form (like trade secrets based on know how) and may have a large tacit component." (p. 2)

Christensen (2003) defines technology as,

> "...the process that any company uses to convert inputs of labor, materials, capital, energy, and information into outputs of greater value. For the purposes of predictably creating growth, treating 'high tech' as different from 'low tech' is not the right way to categorize the world. Every company has technology, and each is subject to these fundamental forces." (p. 39)

Porter (1985) insists that,

> "Technological change is one of the principal drivers of competition. It plays a major role in industry structural change, as well as in creating new industries. It is also a great equalizer, eroding the competitive advantage of even well-entrenched firms and propelling others to the forefront. Many of today's great firms grew out of technological changes that they were able to exploit. Of all the things that can change the rules of competition, technological change is among the most prominent." (p. 164)

Understanding Technology Assets

Prahalad and Hamel emphasize the importance of integrating technology assets in order to develop the core competencies of the organization; *"core competencies are the collective learning in the organization; especially how to coordinate diverse production skills and integrate multiple streams of technologies"* (Prahalad and Hamel, 1990). But they do not detail what these streams of technologies are.

In their 1994 book, *Competing for the Future*, these same authors state that, *"a core competence is a tapestry, woven from the threads of distinct skills and technologies. ... Many companies have had difficulty blending the multiple streams of science or technology that comprise their heritage into new, higher-order competencies"* (Hamel and Prahalad, 1994, p.214). Again, they identify the importance of technologies, but assume that the manager will be able to identify all of the streams of technology that are important to his business.

Sharif (1995 and 1999) suggests that the streams of technology referred to by Prahalad and Hamel, fall into four major categories, and that mastering these technological assets is essential for competitively positioning a company (Figure 13.1). These comprise the "THIO Framework":

* Technoware—object-embodied physical facilities
* Humanware—person-embodied human talents
* Inforware—record-embodied codified knowledge
* Orgaware—organization-embodied operational schemes

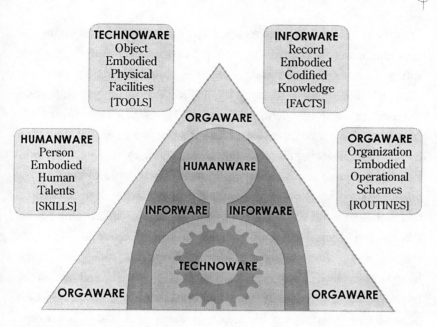

Figure 13.1 There are four technological components that play an essential role in creating and establishing a competitive position for a company. *(Sharif, 1995)*

Technoware refers to equipment, laboratories, and other assets that a company can acquire or create, to assist in creating a product or offering a service. Humanware refers to the capabilities of the people in the organization, and their ability to apply those capabilities in a productive manner. Inforware is the knowledge that is encoded in documents and processes, and that are accessible to the organization. Finally, orgaware describes the capabilities of the organization that are derived from its structure and the processes that determine how it operates.

Christensen and Overdorf (March-April 2000) wrestle with this same issue of defining the valuable assets of an organization when they discuss its resources, processes, and values. They emphasize that the capabilities of new companies are often concentrated in their people (i.e. humanware), because operational processes and organizational values have not yet had time to form. The resources of a start-up company may also include technoware in the form of unique equipment or patent protection on a new technology. Christensen and Overdorf's "processes" are an expression of Sharif's orgaware, in that they refer to the valuable capabilities of the organization as unique from both individual people and specific equipment. Their "values" capture the organization's analysis of the industry and market (i.e. inforware) to determine what they will specialize in. Subramaniam and Youndt (2005) also recognize the importance of humanware and emphasize that it is one of the essential ingredients for enabling radical innovation in an organization. They go on to state that the social relationships between people are an equally important ingredient for innovation – a.k.a. orgaware or social capital. Finally, their research indicates that patents and historical knowledge/information within the organization create organizational capital (i.e. inforware) that is an essential ingredient for enabling incremental innovation of existing products and services. The technology start-ups in Silicon Valley are classic examples of the importance of humanware at the beginning of a venture. The algorithms that established Google as the leading search engine in the world were created and implemented by its two founders, Larry Page and Sergey Brin. In the beginning, their expertise was the most important ingredient in making the company successful. However, over time, that skill and knowledge is not sufficient to grow and operate the business. The company must add organizational capabilities, supporting technologies, and protection of their proprietary information.

In their report on the need for innovation in America, the Council on Competitiveness (December 2004) emphasized the differences between small start-up and large established companies, specifically that small companies rely on the depth of expertise of individuals (humanware) while larger companies rely on the capabilities of the organization (orgaware), and often lack the ability to access unique individual expertise.

Sharif also accepts that there are financial and natural resources available which are not necessarily related to technology. The importance of natural and financial resources was also emphasized by Daniel Bell in describing the evolution of society from its agricultural roots, through its 19th century manufacturing foundation, to the more recent post-industrial or information economy (Bell, 1973). The pattern of this evolution is shown in Figure 13.2.

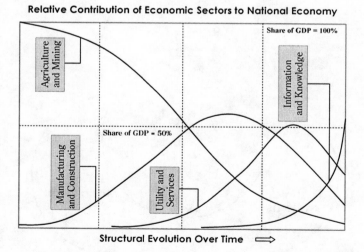

Figure 13.2 The contribution of specific resources and industries to the social economy has evolved over time.

Leonard-Barton (1992) suggests that there are 4 dimensions (or assets) that make up the knowledge-set that enables technological innovation (Figure 13.3). These are:

- Skills and Knowledge Base—knowledge and skill embedded in employees (i.e. Humanware)
- Technical Systems—knowledge embedded in technical systems (i.e. Technoware)
- Managerial Systems—formal and informal ways of creating knowledge (i.e. Orgaware)
- Values and Norms—traditions from the founders (i.e. Inforware)

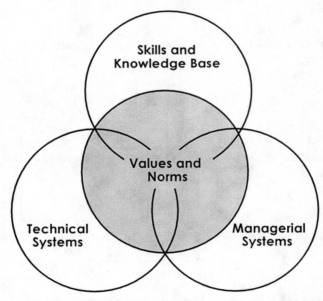

Figure 13.3 Leonard-Barton presents four dimensions of knowledge that contribute to organizational capabilities. *(Leonard-Barton, 1992)*

Each of the above models of technological assets presents them as interlocking or interdependent. The authors emphasize that an organization needs all of them if it is to be successful. Different types of industries and competitors may need them in different proportions, but few, if any, industries totally omit any one category. The balance between these assets also varies over time as a company or industry matures or is transformed by changes in its social or technical environments.

Acquiring Technology Assets

"For the past 25 years, we have optimized our organizations for efficiency and quality. Over the next quarter century, we must optimize our entire society for innovation." (Council on Competitiveness, 2004).

As industry and business have evolved, so have the means of acquiring technology to improve the effectiveness and productivity of human economic endeavors. Chandler (2001) identified the essential role of an "integrated learning base" in supporting the long-term success of a company's innovation programs. He studied the emergence of the consumer electronics and computer industries to determine why some companies were extremely successful in the short-term, but completely lost their position over time. The learning base, to which he refers, is synonymous with the acquisition of new technologies and internal human expertise in applying these technologies. The ability to apply these within a company was one significant differentiator between those companies that survived as producers of electronics, and those that have failed, because they had no internal, integrated competitive advantage. Chandler offers RCA as a classic example of this pattern of growth and decline. RCA held patents for a number of important electronic components and manufacturing methods. However, instead of developing internal capabilities to turn these into products, the company chose to make its money by licensing these patents to other manufacturers. As a result, RCA never developed their own internal expertise with the technology, and when advances came, they came from other companies; leaving RCA holding the rights to outdated technology. It was primarily the Japanese companies that had licensed RCA IP who developed the next generation of technologies and methods, and used them to pull the entire electronics industry away from American companies and into Japanese companies (Chandler, 2001).

In a knowledge economy, the ability to acquire, organize, and apply new knowledge, is an essential ingredient in effective innovation. Christensen and Raynor (2003) state that, *"corporate IT systems and the CIOs who administer them, figure among the most important contributors to failure in innovation"* (p.89). They emphasize that ready access to useful and customized information is a prerequisite for growing and changing the organization. Inforware is not just a controlled body of knowledge that enters with a new employee, nor is created through internal activities. Rather, it is a global environment that extends far beyond the boundaries of the organization. Ingesting and managing as much inforware and technoware as possible is an important part of stimulating the innovation process. This occurs by sending employees to trade shows, industry trade publications, experimenting with competitors' products, looking for inspiration in other industries, and a number of similar approaches to information acquisition.

Technoware is often seen as being the most sophisticated, because it has the power to do more work. Its efficiency in reducing materials and energy, its ability to contain self-guidance and control, and its ease of use and reduced impact on the environment, place it in the limelight of executive attention. But without humanware, this technoware is nonfunctional and useless. Though technoware often contains encoded humanware, it still requires human control and application, which requires human knowledge and skill. Additionally, Orgaware is the structure that is able to bring together the right technology and human skills with a market opportunity. Shifting IBM from a company primarily focused on computer hardware to one centered on services, required pulling together all four of the resources we have identified. They had to master the technology of the new open systems environment, which required applying their humanware expertise, technoware capabilities, and inforware licenses. They also had to recreate the organization so that it could operate effectively around services.

Start-up	Expansion	Consolidation	Leadership
Humanware Human resources are dominant. Values are beginning to form.	**Technoware** Acquisition of technology resources to expand the business and improve productivity.	**Inforware** Understanding of competitive environment and selection of identity based on values.	**Orgaware** Creation of organizational structure and processes.
Competitive advantage stems from the unique skills of individuals and small groups.	Technology assets and equipment add to the competencies of the people and expand the market reach of the company.	Mastery of information about the industry, customers, suppliers, and government lead to specialization.	Competency focuses on the creation of effective organizational structures and the alignment of business processes.
Organization has minimal established capabilities to support competencies.	Technology assets create an initial foundation for corporate capabilities beyond human capital.	Organization establishes processes to govern its resources and to allow them to become independent of uniquely talented individuals.	Organization applies its significant resources in accordance with the business processes and organizational structures that encode its operations.

(left axis: Competencies; right axis: Capabilities; diagonal label: Competencies & Capabilities Ratio)

Leonard-Barton (1992)

Skills & Knowledge	Technical Systems	Values and Norms	Managerial Systems

Christensen & Overdorf (2000)

Resources (Human)	Resources (Technology)	Values	Processes

Subramaniam & Youndt (2005)

Human Capital	Organizational Capital	Organizational Capital	Social Capital

Figure 13.4 Different technology assets make different types of contributions to the growth and competitiveness of a company as it moves through its lifecycle.

Figure 13.4 brings together the concepts presented by multiple authors to illustrate how each of them describes a similar phenomenon. These assets are aligned with the business growth phase; showing which asset is dominant during each phase of the company's lifecycle. During the start-up phase of a company, the humanware assets are the most important ("skills and knowledge" in Leonard-Barton and "resources" in Christensen & Overdorf). The unique skills of individuals are usually the foundations of the company's ability to compete in an industry. As the company expands, it uses its financial capital to purchase technoware that will allow it to extend the productivity of is humanware and reach a larger market ("technical systems" in Leonard-Barton and "resources" in Christensen & Overdorf). As it runs into stiff competition and its expansion carries it into areas that it cannot excel at, the organization realizes the need to consolidate. It must apply inforware about the market, customers, suppliers, and competitors, to determine what its unique place should be. This selection leads to a definition of its values and norms; the definition of what it will pursue and what its measures of success will be. If the company survives, it can potentially enter the market leadership phase of its lifecycle. In this phase, its orgaware is most important. The creation of an organizational structure that can operate the business independent of the individual humanware and technoware assets that were the foundations of the company is essential ("managerial systems" in Leonard-Barton and "processes" in Christensen & Overdorf).

Throughout this evolution, as a category of technological assets moves from a dominant position to a supporting position, it also moves from being a competitive competency of the organization to being an operational capability. These assets are always important, but they become woven into the fabric of the company, to use Prahalad's analogy, and are part of the stable foundation of capabilities, rather than the front-end transformative force of the organization.

Application to Global Competition

The four categories of technology assets are essential resources, both in defending current market positions, and in usurping those positions from competitors. Burgelman asserts that, *"From a competitive strategy point of view, technology can be used defensively to sustain achieved advantage in product differentiation or cost, or offensively as an instrument to create new advantage in established lines of business, or to develop new products and markets."* (Burgelman, 2004, p.143) Having achieved an advantage, technology assets are one essential ingredient in defending that position. Operational efficiencies are necessary, but these can be copied. The earlier quote from the U.S. Council on Competitiveness emphasized the need for innovation to remain competitive, and their report focused on the application of new technology and investment in R&D as a key part of innovativeness.

Christensen and Raynor (2003) attempt to identify actions that senior executives must take to lead this innovation. These actions align very well with the THIO framework that is at the center of this paper. First, executives should stand astride of the interface between sustaining and disruptive innovation for their organization. They should examine the threats of new technology (study and apply technoware) and the need to maintain the capabilities of the current organization (foster humanware). Second, they should champion new processes for generating disruptive growth (advancing orgaware). Third, they should sense when circumstances are changing and teach others to recognize these signs as well (monitoring inforware and mentoring humanware).

Von Hippel (2002 and 2005) and Chesbrough (2003) both point to an additional dimension of this model for managing innovation, one that extends beyond the boundaries of the company. Von Hippel points out that there are "leading-edge users" of every product. These people and organizations press the product to its limit, and often end up inventing modifications that are beyond what is delivered in the original product. As the broader consumer base for these products evolves, it will also discover a need for the modifications pioneered by leading-edge users. Therefore, a company needs to tap into these leading-edge users, create partnerships with them, and bring their modifications into the product research and design process. Chesbrough's ideas concerning "open innovation" talk to the need to leverage the capabilities of multiple organizations to create new products. He has observed that no company possesses the expertise necessary to innovate in all of the domains that apply to its products. Therefore, partnerships are necessary to maintain a lead over more insular competitors. These ideas extend the management and optimization of the THIO framework beyond the boundaries of a single company.

Early Starter Advantage

Technological advancements form S-curves in which early applications provide small, incremental improvements, but these soon lead to significant or exponential improvements. During this exponential phase, it is tempting to believe that the technology will continue to improve business operations, productivity, efficiency, and cost savings at this rate. But, as the potential within each improvement is realized, its contributions taper off significantly to an incremental tail. When an industry is in a stagnant phase, it will remain in the incremental improvement tail for a significant period. Luckily, complex organizations have a number of opportunities to apply new technology assets and to jump onto the early phases of a new S-curve (Moore, 2005).

This makes it very important for a company or a country to adopt and apply new technologies early enough that the explosive financial benefits are still available to pay for start-up costs, which may be significant. If a company or country waits too long to apply a new technology, then it may find itself in a position where the profits available cannot overcome the start-up costs.

Once a company is established in an industry, it can benefit from multiple waves of technological improvement. Moore (2005) points to the importance of applying innovative technologies throughout the life-cycle of the company. During some phases, it is possible to innovate in the technoware components of the product. During others, it is possible to innovate in the orgaware/production processes. At other times, it may be necessary to innovate in the humanware domain.

Innovation may emerge in many different parts of the organization, but it is unlikely that transformative changes will be continuous in any one area. Instead, disruptions in one area will be followed by stability and standardization to make those changes into a repeatable part of the organization's operations. While this standardization is occurring, disruptive innovation may emerge in one of the other domains that drive productivity and competitiveness (Christensen, 1999). Microsoft has experienced the early starter advantage and has had to wrestle with the disruptions that have occurred within and around its operating system business. Having successfully captured the desktop operating system market, Microsoft still had no control over the evolution of the definition of the operating system from the customer's perspective. Companies such as Qualcomm and Netscape extracted the email client and the web browser from university labs and introduced them to Windows customs. Microsoft missed the opportunity to introduce these tools themselves, and had to catch-up to the idea that they should reside side-by-side with every copy of the operating system. More recently, this early starter is facing the same challenges from search engines, media management programs, media editing suites, blogging tools, and a growing list of contenders who hope to create the next ubiquitous tool for the Windows environment.

Late Starter Advantage

Not all industries require a major investment to enter—i.e., they do not have a significant barrier to competitive entry (Porter, 1985). When this is the case, it is possible for a late starter in the field to have an advantage over early starters. Early starters typically pay a premium price for equipment that is just being created to take advantage of technological advancements. Early starters also take the largest risks in predicting market demand and experimenting with new production processes. Since technoware changes so rapidly, it is possible that the early starter will spend significant money and time pursuing failed products and markets. This may make it possible, even advantageous, for another company to start later, but hit the right market with the right product the first time out. Under these conditions, the late starter may outperform the early starter and capture a dominant position in the market (Markides & Geroski, 2005). Apple's iPod is a fantastic example of this approach. They entered the MP3 player market five years after many of the early starters. They had the advantage of understanding the approaches of dozens of existing competitors, and most of the necessary technology had already been created. Apple brought two new ingredients to the MP3 device—a massive internal hard drive that could store thousands of songs, and a superior user interface that appealed to a larger portion of the consumer market. These two advantages allowed them to consolidate a fractured market, capture 70% of the business, and redefine what an MP3 player should be.

Conclusion

In this paper, we have attempted to clearly identify the types of technology assets that a company must acquire and apply in order to be successful in the marketplace. Numerous authors have talked about the importance of managing technologies and "weaving streams of technology", without explicitly defining these technologies. Referring back to Christensen's definition of technology as *"the process that any company uses to convert inputs of labor, materials, capital, energy, and information into outputs of greater value"* (Christensen, 2003), we suggest that managers must consider much more than just traditional R&D and the acquisition of new equipment that represent "hard technology". Rather, a manager must leverage the power of humanware, technoware, inforware, and orgaware as described in this paper. Further, we believe that each of these plays a dominant role during a different phase of a company's lifecycle. As an asset moves from a dominant position to a supporting position, it moves from a differentiating competency to an operational capability. A company cannot survive without creating a strong foundation of capabilities. But capabilities can often be duplicated by competitors, so it is difficult for them to continue to provide a competitive advantage. Therefore, a company must continue to innovate with new technology assets.

14

THE INNOVATION-CENTRIC
COMPANY

The ability to manage innovation successfully is one key to the success of companies like Dell, GE, and Microsoft. In some cases, innovation is synonymous with research. In others, it is the application of existing ideas to new problems. GE's research labs practice innovation when they create new synthetic materials that can become part of medical implants. Microsoft practices innovation when it recognizes the importance of search technology, and engineers it into the operating system. In both cases, the companies recognize that the future is not a copy of the past and they must take action to insure that they are a prominent player in the new structure of things.

Every company faces a unique set of challenges when gearing itself up for innovation. These challenges stem from the current position in the market, historical processes, internal capabilities, leadership support, and available budgets.

Specific Management Challenges

To whom should the responsibility for innovation fall? It cannot be the responsibility of everyone in the organization because that would leave no one to handle all of the other operations of the company. But, it cannot be treated as an island separated from the rest of the company either. Innovation will involve a new way of thinking for people across the organization. It is something that must be supported and communicated from the top of the organization to the bottom. Is an executive level necessary? Can corporate innovation be accomplished without the direct support of a corporate executive?

Who does innovation? If everyone will be the recipient of new processes, equipment, and tools, then who is responsible for creating these and identifying the best application? Is a research laboratory the best environment for creating innovation that will be applied within the company? Or are the internal halls of the company the best source of improved ideas?

Must a company choose between innovation and stability? Can a company provide employment, process, and cultural stability to meet the security needs of employees; while at the same time, innovating to remain at the head of the industry? Constant change is destabilizing and demoralizing to a large number of people. They seek jobs that are secure, stable, and repetitive. Many people need to be able to master the processes they are responsible for, rather than operating in a changing environment that they will never master or even fully understand.

Must a company be innovative alone? Should innovation be carried out internally within the company and shielded from the eyes of everyone else in the industry? Or can a company form unique partnerships that will share in innovative changes? In the latter case, the sustaining advantage of innovation comes from the inability of competitors to duplicate the combination of skills and the processes themselves.

Innovation Office

To become masters of innovation, organizations must make some basic changes to their structure of responsibility. The first of these is to establish an Innovation Office. This organization is charged, not with originating all innovations, but with motivating, tracking, managing, and measuring innovation across the company. Intel Corporation has recently created the corporate position of Chief Technology Officer to assist in this process. Patrick Gelsinger, the first corporate-wide CTO, is responsible for overseeing the work of the research and laboratory organizations. He is expected to keep those organizations focused on creating products that are aligned with the company's strategic vision and mission—to become a hub in which computing and communications technologies can merge to create products that are radically more powerful than those that exist today. Gelsinger's organization is not responsible for marketing Pentium chips or pressing into the cellular telephone market. Instead, the CTO office must strive toward a future in which an Intel product is at the center of new devices and capabilities that include both communication and computation. The integrated cell phone and PDA is an early version of these devices, but certainly not the culmination of the vision.

Innovation as Core

Companies have historically considered the product to be the core of their business. This has been followed by "service as core" and "process as core". A product-centric company may be something like a mid-20th century General Motors Company. The core of their business was focused on the production of the automobile. Everything within the company was structured to ensure that the automobile contained the performance, style, quality, and price that met the customer's needs.

A service-centric company has a broader perspective in which it may provide a product, but it also sees itself as meeting the larger needs of its customers. A service-centric automobile company would not limit its offerings to the automobile; but would expand these to include more of the customer's needs. An automobile-buying customer requires financing to be able to afford the product, and that financing includes a profit margin. Therefore, the late century GM also provided financial services, insurance, title application, license transfer, and any other services that make it easier for the customer to buy an automobile, while also providing additional profits for the company.

A process-centric company may see the customer as a person who has a constant, life-long need for transportation. That person needs to buy an automobile along with the service components. But, they also need transportation when the automobile is being repaired. Since repairs can be done at any number of shops, the GM dealer must provide an incentive to bring the customer to the dealership for repairs. One of those incentives is the loaner car and the shuttle service. These ensure that the owner of a GM automobile has a transportation solution, at all times, during the life of the vehicle. It also builds a relationship that is designed to bring the customer right back to the dealer for the next automobile purchase; preferably a lifetime of purchases.

In an innovation-centric company, the goal is to meet the needs of the customer today, and those that have yet to be imagined in the future. A company must demonstrate that their innovation moves them from a customer's current needs to their future needs before the customer gets there. Customers will learn which companies can only satisfy today's problems and which are already imagining and solving the problems they will have in the future. The innovation-centric company is establishing itself as a lifelong partner. GM's OnStar system can be cast in this innovation-centric light. As people find themselves more independent and disconnected from each other, they learn that they can no longer count on other motorists to render assistance. Therefore, OnStar is a GM innovation that meets the needs of a large part of the automobile customer-base, before the customer's realize that they need it. Like cell phones, the item moves from luxury to necessity as customers catch up with the innovation that has already been offered by GM.

Companies that are serious about innovation must focus themselves around the needs of the future. They must tie the organization to the source of innovation and structure the company such, that they are extracting the maximum value from innovation as quickly as possible.

Flexible Workforce

Thriving and surviving in an innovation-centric company is not something that is natural and easy for many of today's employees. Creating a culture and a workforce that is functional and motivated in such an environment is a major undertaking. Both the company and the employees must build a relationship that grows stronger, because they know how to evolve and change together. The company must be able to teach employees to thrive in the new environment, and the employees must be willing to trade old behaviors for new. Because this transition is difficult, employees who make the change should be more valuable to the company. Perhaps a relationship based on flexibility, adaptation, and innovation can become the foundation for lifelong employment. McFarland Strategy Partners teaches companies that, *"The best way to grow a business is to grow the people. It just doesn't make sense to be replacing people all the time."* (Kurtz, 2004)

In the 19th and 20th centuries, labor struggled to build a foundation for stable employment based on unchanging responsibilities and processes. Someone who could master a specific step in the production process was more valuable as long as that step never changed. In the 21st century, that stability may be based on flexibility. The value to the company is not in the person's ability to become a master at one task; but rather, they are valuable because they have the ability to flex, grow, and change, to master a wide variety of tasks placed before them. Though they may never master one job, they are able to become competent at many successive jobs. People with this flexibility in an innovation-centric company cannot be eliminated because flexibility coupled with competence is too valuable to waste.

Innovation Partnerships

As described earlier, innovation and the mastery of technology does not respect organizational or international boundaries. An innovation-centric company cannot limit itself to people and processes that reside within a specific region, facility, or company. Leaders in innovation must be able to draw innovation into synergistic relationships from any number of sources around the planet.

Managing innovation will be synonymous with managing multi-company teams that cross geographic and international boundaries. They are not bound together by their physical addresses, community history, or even professional specialty. Instead, they are bound together by their faith in a vision of the future, and their eagerness to create something that does not yet exist. In such an environment, the issues like "not invented here", are less an issue because everyone is looking at how the invention can be applied or how it leads to something new that will be invented here. When the allegiance is to a vision or ideal, then issues of company origins and physical location are not important; as long as the partnership can enable progress better than a single in-house effort.

Innovation-centric companies require innovation-centric people. Innovation management is not about controlling and standardizing people and processes, but about enabling and optimizing them. The responsibility of the manager is to cultivate, train, recruit, and unite people to continually improve the innovation process of the combined partnership.

15

DECISION MAKING:
THEORIES AND PROCESSES

or an organization of any type to function, there must be decisions. As organizations become more complex, the number of people empowered to make these decisions and their perspective on the issues involved becomes larger. The organizational leader may see decisions as a means of growing the company, serving the shareholders, or overcoming the competition. An accountant looks at the financial side of each decision, seeking to maximize gain or minimize loss. A management scientist may use mathematical techniques to manipulate quantitative measures of the organization. A strategist sees the long future of the organization and makes decisions that favor the desired future rather than the present situation. A human resources professional weighs the impact that decisions have on individuals and groups of people within the organization. An ethicist seeks the right and moral path through a series of actions. And a technologist may see the importance of technology in the organization, pursuing more of it with the faith that additional technology will deliver productivity.

Authors who write in this area, recognize that the subject of decision making has become significantly more broad and complex that when it first emerged. They confess that this makes it difficult to identify the outer boundaries of the subject and turn their attention to the key processes, perspectives, and tools at the center (Jennings and Wattman, 1998). In this chapter, we will take a similar tact in enlightening the subject. Each section below deals with a major thrust in decision making, and attempts to lay a foundation from which the reader can build in a number of directions through additional study. Wheelwright and Makridakis (1985) delivered a leading work on the subject of forecasting. In that book, they created three useful categories for the forecasting techniques in use at the time—Quantitative, Technological, and Judgmental. We will use this as a structure for the chapter.

General Decision Making Model

Berry argues that there is a common general approach to decision making, and that enhanced group communication can contribute to this (Berry 2006). Nutt (1998) suggests that the process of decision making is well understood and was established by a number of studies beginning with Mintzberg's in 1976. Jennings and Wattman (1998) also summarize the work of Mintzberg, Duru, Raisinghani, and Theoret (1976) in which those authors attempted to create a generalized model of the decision making process. In that early study, the authors extracted the decision making process from 25 different organizations, and attempted to create one model that expressed all of them appropriately. The result was a three phase model with seven major steps embedded in it (Figure 15.1).

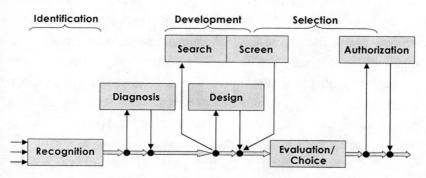

Figure 15.1. A general model of strategic decision making.
(Jennings and Wattman 1998)

During the first phase, situations that require decision making are identified. These are opportunities, problems, or crises that require action for the organization to benefit. In the second phase, a number of solutions to the problem are developed. Elaborations of the problem are created, and the ability of each possible solution to satisfy specific issues is identified. In the final phase, one or more solutions are selected—a decision is made. If we retain this general framework for reference as we review the methods through the paper, we see that it does indeed provide a structure the goes beyond any single method. However, each of the specialized methods provides more depth or detail in areas that are crucial to the domains for which that method was developed.

Quantitative Decision Making

Scientific Management

Fredrick Taylor should lead off the section on quantitative decision making. He published is work, *The Theory of Scientific Management,* in 1911, and has had a tremendous impact on the conduct of business throughout the industrial age and into the information age. Taylor prescribed a very different process of assigning work to individuals; one that was originally seen as a threat to the established processes and organizations. Rather than allowing the workers and supervisors to select the people and tools for each job, Taylor sought to analyze the problem and prescribe the most effective approach to the job. This moved some degree of expertise from those doing the work to those managing the work. It also opened the door for the growth of the "analyst" in business. In addition to managers/owners and workers, there was now a place for a third party who would study the business, design optimum approaches, and prescribe them for execution. In many ways, Taylor's methods were simply an implementation of the theories of Adam Smith. He sought a way to make people and organizations more productive.

In his own words, Taylor describes the process as:

"First, they [managers] develop a science for each element of a man's work, which replaces the old rule-of-thumb method.

Second, they scientifically select and then train, teach, and develop the workman; whereas in the past, he chose his own work and trained himself as best he could.

Third, they heartily cooperate with the men so as to ensure all of the work being done in accordance with the principles of the science which has been developed.

Fourth, there is an almost equal division of the work and the responsibility between the management and the workmen. The management takes over all work for which they are better fitted than the workmen; while in the past, almost all of the work and the greater part of the responsibility were thrown upon the men.

It is this combination of the initiative of the workmen, coupled with the new types of work done by the management, which makes scientific management so much more efficient than the old plan." (Taylor, 1998)

Though the efficiencies described here seem obvious and self-justifying, they redefined the relationship between management and workers. In this new definition, it was assumed that management had a better ability to determine the best way of conducting work than did the people who actually did the work. This perspective was not welcome at the time, nor is it always welcome in organizations today. All workers want to believe that they own their jobs and know best how to do them. But, transferring ownership for their actions to the organization itself, through the agency of management, disempowers them, threatens to make them interchangeable, and removes their leverage in running the organization. Today, we continue to balance the ownership of a job between the worker (empowerment) and the organization (productivity). We recognize that both add value to the process, but must continue to overcome differences in the motives of the two parties.

Statistical Analysis

Though scientific management contains many quantitative parts, like the weight of pig iron in a given size of shovel, statistical analysis takes this significantly further by working directly and solely with numbers. It attempts to extract meaning from large amounts of data about a given population. It also applies considerable focus to determining what the appropriate population for measurement should be. The statistician discovers relationships that exist within a population, and identifies effective processes to be applied to the population. This method does not deal directly with individuals. After assigning an individual to a category, statistical analysis prescribes the same actions for everyone in that category. These techniques for making decisions are the core foundation upon which insurance products are based. Without these, the practice of selling insurance would be highly subjective and would almost certainly devolve into illegal and unethical practices to prevent companies from going out of business.

In the real world, populations of interest are complex and require much more than a standard normal distribution to describe them. Multiple equations are needed to characterize the population and techniques are needed to blend these together at threshold points. Table 1 summarizes some of the statistical methods that have emerged as solutions to specific types of problems. Information like this, serves as a cookbook for applying statistics to problems that have the same form as many others in a class that have been studied and categorized.

Table 1. Some standard statistical distributions and the class of problems for which they are used.

Statistical Distribution	Type of Problem
Uniform	Binary decision on probability of success or failure. Source of random numbers between 0 and 1 that is used to drive many of the other methods
Normal	Dispersion errors around a central average; such as the errors around the aimpoint of a bomb
Weibull	Time to failure for a piece of equipment
Exponential	Inter-arrival times of customers at a constant rate
Gamma	Time to serve a customer
Beta	Proportion of defective items in a shipment
Bernoulli	Success or failure of a specific experiment
Poisson	Number of items in a batch of random size
Empirical	Curves custom fitted to collected data

Source: Law and Kelton, 1991

Expert Systems and AI

Artificial Intelligence and Exert Systems blend judgment and quantitative methods. Associating cause and effect is largely an extraction of the judgment of an expert. But, organizing that in a form that software can process requires quantification. Expert knowledge is usually ranked or scored so that those numbers can be processed through mathematical equations to find minimum, maximum, average, most likely, and other quantitative points.

The expert knowledge of the system is stored in a distinct knowledge base. It is removed from the inference engine that reasons or calculates over the data set. The goal is to provide a universal inference engine that can process information in any number of expert domains (Figure 15.2).

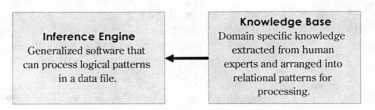

Figure 15.2 General structure of an expert system (a.k.a. Production System).
(Russell and Norvig, 1995)

Often, the software can be adjusted by a human expert or programmer when the decisions are not coming out as expected. Many AI techniques include a learning phase in which these adjustments are done. Throughout the history of AI, we have come to appreciate the complexity of the knowledge that humans reason on, and the fuzzy understanding that an expert has for how he or she is processing that knowledge. As a result, we tend to create AI systems that mimic the results of human decision making, rather than the exact process that a human uses.

Financial Decision Making

Financial decision making focuses on accounting or budgeting methods. Accounting methods attempt to determine the benefits of an investment or expenditure, often comparing current outlays with future revenues. The Payback Method simply determines when an outlay will have earned back the investment that was sunk into it. For example, in acquiring a business, the Payback Method calculates when the revenues from that business acquisition will equal the amount paid to acquire it.

The Net Present Value method takes this logic a step further. It recognizes that capital is not free to the company that uses it. The money must be borrowed from an outside source or from an inside alternative investment. This incurs a cost of using that capital. The NPV method looks at the value of that money today and compares it with the value of applying it to an alternative investment. If the investment returns a higher rate than the money can be borrowed for, then it is a viable investment. This method also allows comparisons of different types of investments. All possible uses of the money are boiled down into their rate of return (Brigham and Houston, 1999).

Budgeting is a financial decision method that looks at the expected costs to operate in the coming year, as compared to the costs experienced in previous years. Its goal is to establish a pattern of spending that allows the company to grow, but that prevents it from overspending its money. Budgets are often enforced by creating management incentive schemes to hold on to money when it does not appear to promise a high return (Jennings and Wattman, 1998).

Real Options

Real options are an attempt to apply a financial options method to the acquisition or optioning of assets that are not as clearly defined as financial instruments. In most cases, a real option is based on the Black-Scholes Merton (BSM) equation that is very popular for valuing stock options. This method for decision making is described in detail in a separate chapter of this book.

Operations Research & Management Science

Moder and Elmaghraby (1978) define operations research as, using *"the method of science to understand and explain phenomena of operating systems."* This definition separates the field from other sciences that focus on unique properties of the natural world. It also separates OR from most business practices by the application of a scientific rather than an empirical approach. These authors trace the beginnings of the science from 1935, when the British used scientific methods and experiments to study the use of radio waves for locating aircraft; later to be called radar. During World War II, scientists in the U.K. and the U.S. continued to extend this new science as they applied mathematics, logic, and experimentation to numerous problems in warfare. Immediately following the war, Kimball and Morse wrote an entire book capturing the emergence and evolution of these techniques (Morse and Kimball 1998). Though they were initially applied to military logistics problems, combat operations, weapon design, and ship repair; over time they were adopted by other domains like manufacturing and business management in which they were often labeled "management science".

Mark Eisner of Cornell University defines operations research as, *"the effective use of scarce resources under dynamic and uncertain conditions"* (Postrel, 2004). Just as Fredrick Taylor and Adam Smith sought to improve the productivity of business operations, the field of OR continues to apply mathematical and logical methods toward this end. Some of the methods used are statistics, optimization, queuing theory, game theory, graph theory, and simulation. All attempt to improve decision making by quantifying problems and estimating likely outcomes.

Mathematic Programming

Mathematic programming allows an analyst to specify a problem with an objective function and a set of constraints, as in the general equation shown below. Once this is done, it is possible to solve the equations to identify the maximum or minimum value of the system. When the mathematic functions are all linear (first order) equations, then this is known as linear programming.

$$f(x_1, x_2, \ldots, x_n) = a_1 x_1 + a_2 x_2 + \cdots + a_n x_n + b$$

This method requires that an analyst be able to define the relationships between multiple variables and organize them into an objective for the system. If all problems were both continuous and linear, this process would be relatively easy. Unfortunately, real problems often have higher order effects and discontinuities that require creating multiple equations and solving them piecewise, to arrive at an estimation of the behavior of the system.

Game Theory

Game theory was created by John von Neumann to explore the behavior of systems in which two players are anticipating what the other will do as they make their own decisions. Traditional game theory is a two-person, zero-sum game. This means that it is limited to problems with two players, and that for every point, dollar, or advantage gained by one player, the other player loses an equal amount (Davis, 1983 and Macrae, 1992). Figure 15.3 illustrates a traditional game theory problem in which the "winnings" of each player for a pair of decisions varies based on the decision by each of them.

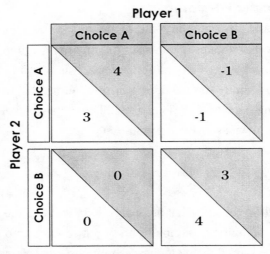

Figure 15.3 Two-person Non-zero Sum Game Theory Proposed by von Neumann.

Unfortunately, few problems in business are so tightly constrained. For example, in the battle of cost conscious shoppers, there are currently three major players—Wal-Mart, Target, and Costco. This cannot be tackled with traditional game theory. Also, shopping does not appear to be a zero-sum game. Certainly, the population has a limit on the amount of money that they can spend. But there is a buffer between the absolute amount of money available and the amount that a person is willing to spend. Advertising and other promotions are often designed to encourage a shopper to spend more than they were originally planning to spend. Therefore, retailers compete to increase the amount spent, not just to redirect it away from competitors and toward their own stores.

John Nash proposed an extension to von Neumann's original game theory that allows the method to be applied to larger numbers of players. In the Nash Equilibrium, all of the players settle into a decision that optimizes each of their returns within the party of players. This allows the method to be extended to more than two players, and allows exploration of non-zero-sum games.

Decision Trees

Decision trees are visual graphs showing a series of potential decisions by players in a system. The decision mechanism for selecting a decision may be deterministic or probabilistic. These are very useful when an analyst does not know how any individual will decide, but does have data about how a population decides. This allows the analyst to calculate the expected outcome of an entire system. Figure 15.4 shows a simple two-step decision tree in which the decision mechanism is probabilistic. Trees can be much larger than this, and may involve deterministic methods for making decisions. Other methods like game theory and expert systems can be structured as decision trees.

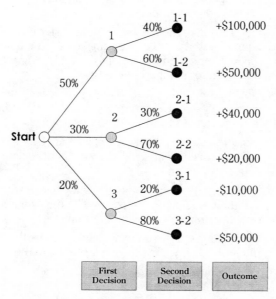

Figure 15.4 Simple two-step, probabilistic decision tree.

Technological

Model Building

A model represents the essential characteristics of a system that we are interested in understanding in greater detail or that we need to communicate to others. A model may be quantitative, but it may also be logical or conceptual. Jennings and Wattman describe eight different types of models that are useful in decision making. These are shown in Table 2.

Table 2. Types of Models Useful for Decision Making

Name	Description
Descriptive	A qualitative description and explanation of the system we are considering, e.g. a word picture of the problem domain.
Predictive	Estimates the future performance, cost, and accuracy of expected values, may be accessed, e.g. data collected over a period of time or area are analyzed to produce the necessary guide values.
Mechanistic	Description of the behavior of the system; given its inputs, outputs, and processing requirements. Such a model is provided by the analysis and design documents produced for computer systems.
Empirical/ Statistical	Obtained by fitting data to mathematical models from existing systems, e.g. regression analysis, finding average figures from groups of like figures.
Steady State	Maps the systems average performance against time, e.g. as above in statistical analysis, but the data are dependent on time.
Dynamic	Represent the fluctuations of performance with time, e.g. the model behaves exactly like the problem domain over the time span of the experiment.
Local	Descriptions of the individual subsystems that form the model, and hence in the aggregate, form the system.
Global	Provide descriptions of the whole of each model, and hence, of the system.

Source: Jennings and Wattman, 1998

System Dynamics

Systems Dynamics was introduced by Jay Forrester as a tool for understanding systems in 1956 (Forrester, 2003). He showed the influence that relationships within a system have on the overall behavior of the system. Of particular importance, was the role played by delay in the system. When an input is changed, it may not impact the output of the system immediately, but may manifest itself much later. This often leads decision makers to assume that some other variable has caused the change. Forrester's models connected cause and effect over time, so that it was clear why a change in the system occurred.

These models also capture the effects of feedback in the model. Certain actions may positively or negatively reinforce behavior in the model. These non-obvious loops can be exposed by the model.

Jennings (1998) suggests that the general process of building a system dynamics model is described in Figure 15.5.

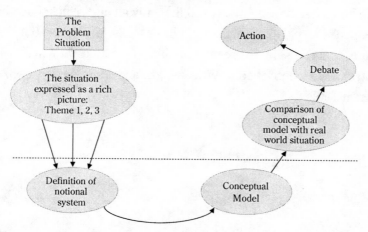

Figure 15.5 Process for constructing and applying a systems model.
(Jennings and Wattman, 1998)

Forecasting

Wheelwright & Makridakis present forecasting as a family of techniques that can be used to predict future events or trends. In their 1985 book, they place all of their techniques in three categories; the same that I have used to organize this paper. Since forecasting techniques fall across all of these categories, I have chosen to summarize the technique in the technology section of this paper, rather than divide them into three pieces for each of the sections.

Forecasting is an organized way of looking at information that is currently available, in order to predict or guess at the future state of a system. Wheelwright points out, that most people are surprised to realize that they do forecasting all the time and even use some of the techniques described in the table. But they do so without realizing that the subject is studied, organized, and improved upon in a systematic manner.

In business, forecasting is used in nearly all disciplines. Each business needs to plan its actions in light of likely future situations, and each uses forecasting to create a roadmap or outline for action. All of the techniques described in Wheelwright and Makridakis (1985) are given in Table 3.

Table 3. Wheelwright and Makridakis' Taxonomy of Forecasting Methods

Approach	Method Groups	Major Methods	Description
Quantitative	Time Series	Naïve	Simple rules, such as forecast equals most recent actual value or equals last year plus 5%
		Decomposition	A data time is broken down into trend, seasonability, cyclicality, and randomness
		Simple Time Series	Forecasts are obtained by averaging (smoothing) past actual values
		Advanced Time Series	Forecasts are obtained as combinations of past actual values and/or past errors
	Explanatory	Simple Regression	Variations in the variable to be forecasted are explained by variations in another variable
		Multiple Regression	Variations in the variable to be forecasted are explained by variations among more than one other variable
		Econometric Models	Systems of simultaneous equations where the interdependence among variables is taken into account
		Multivariate Methods	Statistical approaches allowing predictions through the analysis of multivariate time series data
	Monitoring	Tracking Signals	Nonrandom fluctuations are identified so that a warning signal can be given
Technological	Extrapolation	Delphi	A systematic and rational way of obtaining the intuitive insights of experts, which avoids some of the problems of group meeting
		Trend Extrapolation	Extrapolating the prevailing tendency of a series
		Morphological Research	An enumeration of all possibilities in a way that could facilitate selecting promising future alternatives

Approach	Method Groups	Major Methods	Description
		System Dynamics	An approach based on differential equations that attempt to model the future by extrapolating interacting and nonlinear trends and/or relationships
	Normative	Cross Impact	The interdependence among important future developments is found and used to predict the occurrence of those developments that appear most often
		Pattern	A systematic way of incorporating preferences as a way of forecasting future events
		"La Perspective"	An approach to the long-term, based on the belief that the future is created partly by human actions and partly through uncontrollable events
Judgmental	Individual	Individual Judgment	Intuitive, ad hoc ways of making forecasts
		Multiple Attribute Decision Making	Formalizing forecasting by making explicit subjective probabilities, preference, and the decision process
	Group	Committees	Forecasts made in groups meeting face-to-face and discussing future
		Sales Force Estimates	A bottom-up approach aggregating sales persons' forecasts
		Juries of Executive Opinion	Marketing, production, and finance executives meet and jointly prepare forecasts
	Aggregates	Anticipatory Surveys	Learning about intentions of potential customers through sampling surveys
		Market Research	Finding out customers' preferences through pretesting of new products

Source: Wheelwright and Makridakis, 1985

Linstone's Perspectives

Linstone (1999) maintains that complex systems have three distinct perspectives from which the system can be understood. The *technical* perspective explains how the system operates, what its core parts are, and the machinery or technology that provides this functionality. The *organizational* perspective is how this meets the needs of the group and whether it follows standard operating procedures. The *personal* perspective sees the system as a means to achieving some personal end, identifies the personal benefits, and seeks to elevate self above the group. Figure 15.6 illustrates these three perspectives on a single complex problem.

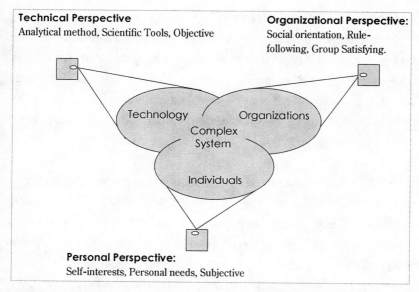

Figure 15.6 Three Perspectives in Decision Making *(Linstone, 1999)*

When making decisions, each of these perspectives is at work manipulating and shading our decisions. Linstone makes it clear that many differences in solutions are driven by differences in perspective, motivation, and mindset. Complex systems usually require the application of multiple people or groups in addressing the problem. These people all see a problem differently and have different tools for understanding and solving it. As a result, each person may be unable to understand the approach of all of the others. Many times, the final result is not understandable to an outside observer because it is a compromise or compilation of the heterogeneous perspectives of many people.

Judgmental

Vigilant Problem Solving

Janis (1989) constructed the vigilant problem solving method for making decisions. He perceived that high quality decisions were negatively impacted by three major constraints—the egocentric, the cognitive, and the affiliative forces on the decision maker. The process he prescribes, attempts to overcome these constraints and achieve better decision results.

Egocentric constraints are those that drive the person to seek personal prestige, to maintain self esteem, and to satisfy personal emotional needs. Cognitive constraints are those that limit the amount of time, expertise, and resources that can be applied to a decision. Affiliative constraints are those that drive people to seek acceptance from the group, to maintain consensus, and to build social support.

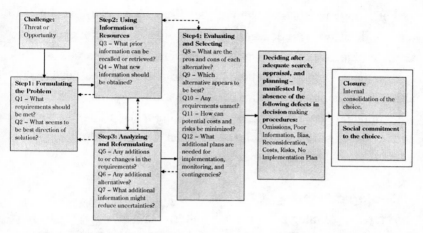

Figure 15.7 Janis' Vigilant Decision Making Process. *(Janis, 1989)*

Janis' decision making model is shown in Figure 15.7. It begins with a challenge, threat, or opportunity that needs to be addressed. The first step is to formulate the problem by identifying the requirements that have to be met and identifying the best direction of a potential solution, i.e. a "top of the head survey of alternatives". Step two is using information resources. Recall information that is available to understand the situation and identify new information that needs to be gathered pertaining to the problem. Step three is analyzing and reformulating the problem and the potential solutions. Did research uncover additional alternatives? What additional information is needed? Have any of the original requirements changed? Step four is evaluating and selecting a solution. Weigh the pros and cons of each alternative. Identify the best option. Identify unmet requirements. Minimize costs and risks. In Janis' process, these four steps all contain feedback loops so that information revealed in one can be used to change the results of a previous step.

Following the four steps and any feedback loops, the next step is to make a decision. The decision should avoid defects like; gross omissions in objectives or alternatives; poor information search; selective bias in processing information; failure to reconsider earlier rejected alternatives; failure to examine major costs and risks; and failure to create a detailed plan for implementation. The decision making process ends with "closure", in which the decision is consolidated, supported internally, and announced externally.

Strategic Planning & Decision Making

Strategic planning is a form of long-term, large-focus decision making. It requires that leaders and groups determine what an organization should be involved in, how it should be structured, and what its strategies should be.

Jennings and Wattman describe strategic planning as determining, *"what activities should the organization be involved in, and how will it compete in its various business areas?"* (Jennings and Wattman, 1985, p.257). They identify three major sectors for the application of strategic planning:

1. Defining mission, objectives, and goals;
2. Responding to the environment; and
3. Leveraging resources of the organization.

Throughout their section on this subject, they refer repeatedly to the work of Henry Mintzberg and summarize his models.

Mintzberg explored deliberate planning in which groups of leaders organize themselves specifically to create a strategic plan for the organization. Considering the history of some of industry's major deliberate planners—e.g. IBM and GM—he is also quite critical of the process, questioning whether it creates real advantage in the market (Mintzberg, 1994).

Mintzberg (2001) explored emergent planning in which strategies are not created immediately and deliberately, but are crafted by the organization and emerge over time as an understanding of the mission and the capabilities becomes clear. Since the business environment and specific situations are constantly evolving and changing, it is essential that strategy have a malleable form. Emergent strategy, or crafted strategy, is one way to address this.

Mintzberg also explored scenario-based planning (1994). Contrary to deliberate strategy development which often requires predicting the future, detaching from the organization, and formalizing a strategy that will not change; scenario-based planning creates strategies in pieces that are aligned with specific scenarios, or cases, that the company may face. Turning to the philosopher Kierkegaard, Mintzberg recognizes that *"Life is lived forward, but understood backward."* As robust as any planning session may be, it cannot really predict or even understand the future. Real understanding comes some time after the events have occurred.

Ketchen et al (2004) frame strategic decision making as managing the "competitive dynamics" of an industry. They focus their attention on decisions to:

1. Enter a new market,
2. Respond to a competitive attack,

3. Pursue growth in existing markets, and
4. Decide whether to compete or cooperate.

They argue that these four questions are central to a company's future and contain the motivators for major strategic decisions.

Rajagopalan, Rasheed, and Datta (1993) conducted a survey of all published papers on strategic decision making from 1981 to 1992. Their analysis led to an integrative framework that characterizes the factors that significantly impact decision making. This framework (Figure 15.8) suggests that there are three major types of input to strategic decision making—environmental, organizational, and decision-specific factors. The process results in two forms of outcome. The process outcome refers to the methods that are selected for arriving as a decision and the characteristics of that method, such as time to a decision. The economic outcome refers to the financial impact that decision processes have had on organizations.

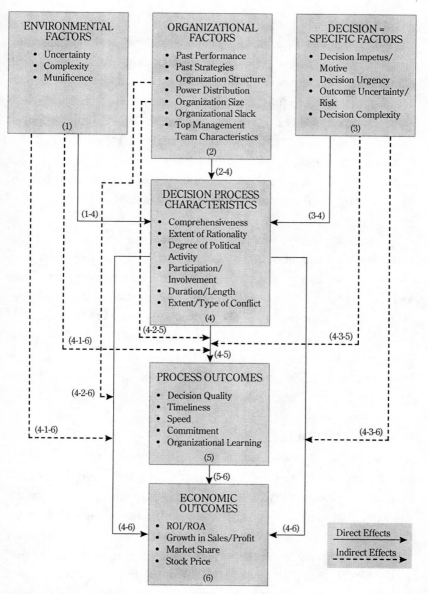

Figure 15.8 Integrative framework of published works on strategic decision making from 1981 to 1992. *(Rajagopalan, Rasheed, and Datta 1993)*

Satisficing

Janis attempted to present a decision making process that could be used to extract the best decision from all of the information available. His model and several others assume that leaders have the time and the inclination to fully explore information before making a decision. Recognizing that this was not realistic, Herbert Simon proposed a bounded rationality model of decision making. He understood that there was far too much information for any person or group to gather and analyze all of it. Therefore, the rationality of a decision is bounded by the subset of information that is collected and analyzed.

Additionally, Simon recognized that decisions are not always optimal, even for a subset of the information available. Rather, most decisions must satisfy a number of stakeholders with different objectives and different perspectives on the issue, such as the three perspectives proposed by Linstone. As a result, most decisions aim to "satisfice" the parties involved. The decision must be satisfactory to all of the stakeholders roughly in proportion to the leverage that those stakeholders have over the decision making process. These concepts won Simon the Nobel Prize in Economics in 1978.

Military OODA Loop

For combat situations, the military has adopted a decision making process created by Korean War fighter pilot, John Boyd. He studied combat situations for years to create the OODA loop process, proposing that all combat decisions be made based on the process of Observe, Orient, Decide, and Act. When first proposed, this method was largely ignored and did not become de rigueur until the mid-1990's (Spinney, 1997). Figure 15.9 illustrates the OODA loop using the graphic created by John Boyd and presented at his last public speaking engagement at Maxwell Air Force Base in 1995.

Boyd's OODA process is cyclical so that it can adjust to the ever changing situation on the battlefield. The opponent is constantly changing his actions to adjust to your actions, which means that your decision processes must react to those changes. *Observation* integrates information from the circumstances you are in and the information that you already have. It also includes information from interacting with the environment and guidance coming from the orientation phase. *Orientation* integrates observations with the leader's previous experience, new information, genetic heritage, and cultural tradition. All of this is subject to analysis and synthesis. *Decision* selects alternatives and passes the preferred option to action. Once *action* is taken, the OODA process begins again as soon as there is feedback from the action and there are observed facts from the action to be evaluated.

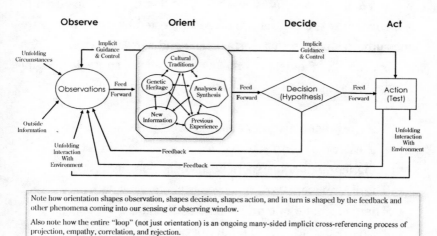

Note how orientation shapes observation, shapes decision, shapes action, and in turn is shaped by the feedback and other phenomena coming into our sensing or observing window.

Also note how the entire "loop" (not just orientation) is an ongoing many-sided implicit cross-referencing process of projection, empathy, correlation, and rejection.

From "The Essence of Winning and Losing," John R. Boyd, January 1996.

Defense and the National Interest, http://www.d-n-i.net, 2006

Figure 15.9 John Boyd's Observe-Orient-Decide-Art Loop for Military Decision Making *(Boyd, 1995)*

Current military leaders speak of "getting inside your opponent's decision loop". This refers to our desire to observe, orient, decide, and act faster than the opponent. We are using computer information systems and electronic communications to enable this. Larger and more accurate weapons are not the only means of defeating an opponent. Adjusting actions and making decisions faster can make existing weapons and tactics more effective.

High-Velocity Decision Making

Eisenhardt (1989) studied the methods and effectiveness of decision making within microcomputer companies, which she described as "high-velocity environments". Her study of eight of these companies led her to believe that in rapidly changing industries like microcomputers, rapid decision making is essential, and that the methods used by these companies are contrary to those suggested by a number of previous authors studying more established and slower changing industries. Specifically, she believes that as the speed of strategic decision making increases in these organizations, the following also occur:

- They rely upon greater amounts of real-time information.
- A greater number of alternatives are considered.
- A higher number of experienced counselors are involved.
- There is an increased use of active conflict resolution.
- There is greater integration among decisions.
- Faster decisions lead to higher performance.

Eisenhardt suggests that in high-velocity environments, decision makers integrate more information and use more advisors than in slower or more traditional processes. Moving faster does not necessarily require that decisions be poorly considered or hasty.

Gut Instinct

Gut instinct is a recognized approach to decision making. At one time, this was thought to refer to a person's innate ability to make good decisions based on the "feel" of the situation or information. But, Hayashi presents a more modern and logical explanation, *"People who use their gut are often relying on data that has been digested and stored subconsciously. This is the material that points in a direction. 'Gut instinct' is moving that information to the conscious level and expressing it as a decision. This requires consuming large amounts of information to create the subconscious base"* (Hayashi, 2001).

Like our experiences with the expert systems described above, decision makers often cannot explicitly describe the rules, processes, or clues that are connected to their decision. This inability to formulate a cause has been incorrectly called instinct, when it is probably a map built through extensive experience and learning which is being followed subconsciously by the decision maker. This emphasizes the importance of both extensive experience and extensive learning to create these internal maps.

Burke and Miller (1999) identified five different categories of intuitive decision making based on interviews with sixty executives. Their surveys identified:

* Experience-based decisions involving a "library" of previous experiences that are evaluated in light of current circumstances.
* Affect-initiated decisions based on feelings and emotions concerning a situation.
* Cognitive-based decisions applying skills, knowledge, and training.

- Subconscious mental processing in which the source of information or understanding is not explicitly identified.
- Decisions based on personal or company values and ethics.

Sauter (1999) explored the importance of "intuitive decision making" and the support that computer decision support systems (DSS) can provide to that. She suggested that there are three different types of intuition. The first is "illumination" in which a decision maker suddenly becomes aware of a solution, and the processes toward this decision are completely hidden. The second is "detection", which occurs when the conscious mind is working on another problem, and the subconscious mind is putting together information and answering questions that lead to a decision. The third is "evaluation" in which a person can select the right answer from multiple options. This last type is often used to validate or question a decision that had originally been made analytically. Sauter argues that in modern business environments, leaders do not remain within a single industry long enough to build up an internal repository of knowledge and experience to enable accurate intuitive decision making. Therefore, decision support and data mining systems should be used to augment or validate decisions made by people new to an industry.

Group Decision Making

Group decision making is influenced by variables that transcend individual characteristics and skills. These include group size, relative status of the members, relationships between members, communication patterns and methods, intragroup competitions, shared or competing goals, and degree of locality (Jennings, 1998).

Groups can encourage and bring out unique and diverse solutions. But, they can also work to reinforce the status quo. Janis pointed out that the affiliative constraint was one effect that limits people's ability to think and act objectively (Janis 1989). He studied this effect in events like the bombing of Pearl Harbor, escalation of the Vietnam War, and the Bay of Pigs invasion. His conclusion was that there are three antecedent conditions that rob groups of the benefit of the intelligence of the members. These are:

1. High stress from external threats, with low hope of a better solution than the one offered by the leaders,
2. High group cohesiveness, and
3. Persuasive strength of the group's leader.

Denning and Hayes-Roth (2006) explore the nature of decision making in hastily formed networks of organizations, such as FEMA groups responding to hurricane damaged areas. Those networks lack a great deal of organization and communication protocols that typically evolve within groups over time. In fact, they find that the most important attribute of decision making in this environment is delegation and empowerment. They find that there is:

1. Too much data to aggregate at a single command center,
2. Rapidly changing situations with backlogs of data,
3. No unified perspective on the problem, and
4. No ability to deliver decisions from a single centralized director of the network.

All of these make it difficult for hastily formed networks to operate effectively. Opportunities to train, rehearse, and discuss situations across the organizations that will be formed into a network can improve the performance of the network. It is not necessary that the rehearsal exactly replicates the network that will emerge in an emergency. The act of rehearsing familiarizes people with the issues listed above and allows them to develop more effective methods of working within hastily formed networks.

Role-playing and Wargaming

Mintzberg's basis for scenario-based planning may have had its roots in the ancient practice of role-playing or wargaming a situation. These events force players to act out potential plans and reactions. They place the motivations and the actions they spawn out in the open, so that all parties can analyze and discuss them. In most cases, role-playing brings out knowledge that the players did not know they possessed or triggers reactions that they would not have predicted. In role-playing, all players assume the identity of their part and their thoughts on a situation have to be verbalized. Practitioners find that this often allows them to transcend stereotypes and presumed behaviors, exploring options that do not come out in more passive types of analysis (Abt, 1970; Brewer and Shubik, 1979).

Field Marshall Eric von Manstein, created political wargaming at the opening of WWII. His intention was to use it to understand the reaction of world leaders to the German invasion of Poland. German military officers and politicians assumed the roles of various world leaders and attempted to create appropriate responses that would come from each country (Perla, 1990). As with all role playing and model building, the person assuming the role must attempt to mimic the cultural background and national interests of someone very different from themselves. A German officer playing a British Ambassador often acts more German in his responses than British, or acts the British stereotype that is common among German leaders.

More currently, emergency managers role-play crisis situations around conference tables. They discuss their plans for handling casualties, activating medical personnel, closing city streets, evacuating areas, and dozens of other actions. These desktop wargames allow leaders to think through their own actions and to place them in the context of other organizations with which they will be cooperating.

Environmental Factors

Risk Management
Risk management is used to try to eliminate threats to the success of a project. It focuses on the probability of a negative event occurring, and the impact that a particular event could have on a project or system. Typically, this is illustrated and tracked through the use of a grid that compares these two variables on high and low scales (Figure 15.10).

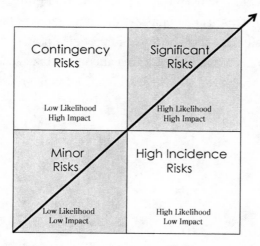

Figure 15.10 Risk management compares likelihood of occurrence with impact of occurrence. *(University of Kent)*

Minor risks are those that are considered unlikely and low impact. In many cases, these are ignored. *Significant* risks are those that are both highly likely and of high impact. These risks are the primary focus of those tracking risks. Risk managers usually develop two types of plans. The first is a response plan in case the significant event does occur. How will the crisis be handled and how will the breadth of impact be minimized? The second is a set of alternatives. Is there a way to eliminate these risks by changing something about the project?

The other two quadrants of the matrix describe risks that have a high likelihood and a low impact (*High Incidence*); or a high impact, but a low likelihood (*Contingency*). These are considered medium-level risks. They need to be managed because they can impact the project, but they are less important than the significant risks.

The risk management quad-chart may also be presented as a grid of scores that allow convenient color coding of the threat of the risk (Figure 15.11). This grid emphasizes the importance of the significant risks in the red areas and the lower importance of minor risks in the green areas. Risk management teams attempt to take actions that can move risks from the red and yellow regions into the green region.

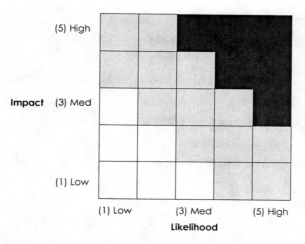

Figure 15.11 Color coded risk grid with scoring in each dimension.

Janis' Constraints

Irving Janis identified three major constraints that influence decision making—cognitive, affliative, and egocentric constraints (Figure 15.12). Each of these arises from a different set of environmental factors.

Cognitive constraints emerge when there is limited time to make a decision. A group will find itself unable to apply all of the information that it has, or to acquire all of the information that it needs. The group may also face this when it has multiple tasks to perform and cannot focus in-depth attention on any one of them. If the group perceives that it has limitations on its ability to collect information, is confused by the complexity of the issue, or has ideological commitments, then it may experience cognitive constraints.

Affliative constraints emerge when members of a group must maintain their power, status, compensation, or social support. Breaking ranks with the group threatens these, and hinders the members from offering solutions that vary from the ideas of the group.

Egocentric constraints are invoked when members have a strong personal motive in a specific decision—such as financial or power opportunities. This also occurs when a group triggers emotional needs or reactions from its members. These emotions can drive the group to seek to satisfy their emotions rather than to find an optimal solution to the problem.

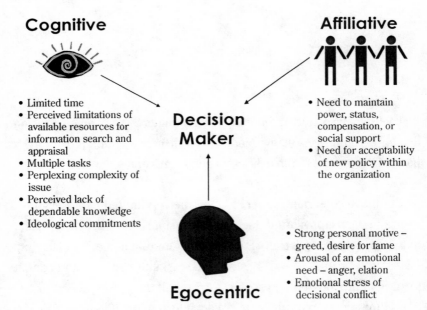

Figure 15.12 Janis' major categories of decision making constraints. *(Based on Janis 1989)*

Hidden Traps

Hammond, Keeney, and Raiffa (1998) identified eight different traps that are hidden in the decision making environment. These hidden traps prevent people from making good decisions and can prevent them from coming to decisions at all. These traps are:

* *Anchoring*—The mind gives disproportionate weight to information that is received first. This early data anchors thoughts and judgments about future information.
* *Status-quo*—Decision makers show a bias toward lanes of action that perpetuate the status quo.
* *Sunk Costs*—People prefer to stick with decisions that have previous sunk costs under the perception that changing a decision is equivalent to abandoning that money or time.
* *Confirming Evidence*—People decide what they want to do and then use information gathering to accumulate the support they need to back that decision.
* *Framing*—Before a decision can be made, the problem must be framed. This initial framework for the problem can distort the purpose of the effort and lead to a decision that optimizes for the frame, but not for the true problem.
* *Overconfidence*—People tend to be overconfident concerning the accuracy of their judgments and estimates. Even though people are very poor at estimation, most individuals believe that they are more accurate than others.
* *Prudence*—Decisions are adjusted toward a more safe result. After an estimate is made, a "just to be safe" buffer is added to increase the likelihood of meeting the need. This often occurs at multiple levels in the decision making process; leading to wildly "over safe" actions.

- *Recallability*—People recall their successes much more vividly than they recall their failures. Therefore, they use this distorted lens when making decisions. They are more likely to remember when they handled a similar situation successfully than when they did so unsuccessfully. This leads to overconfidence in the expected results.

The authors provide examples of each of these hidden traps and successful means of overcoming them. In most cases the solution involves objective and self-depreciating evaluations of the situation and the information at hand.

Conceptual Schema

Shoemaker (1993) presents a conceptual framework of decision making in which the congruency of goals and the efficiency in coordination create four different action sets for the decision maker (Figure 15.13).

Efficiency of Coordination

		High	Low
Congruency of Goals	**High**	Organizational Model	Unitary Actor
	Low	Contextual View	Political Model

Figure 15.13 Shoemakers Conceptual Framework for motivation and communication in decision making. *(Shoemaker, 1993)*

The Unitary Actor has very high goal congruency and coordinative efficiency because he or she is acting alone and is completely aligned with his or her own motives. The organizational model assumes that a group has a high level of goal congruency—they are acting together toward a common goal, but they have a lower level of coordinative efficiency. The Political Model assumes that there are personal forces at work that misalign the goal congruency, but retain high coordination. Finally, the Contextual View assumes that goal congruency and coordinative efficiency are both lacking, because the problem to be solved has its own internal goals, rather than fitting into some larger external goal set.

Cultural Effects

Fons Trompenaars spent fourteen years studying forty-six thousand managers in forty countries. His work led him to create six cultural dimensions that impact the work and decisions of managers (Hampton-Turner and Trompenaars, 2000). Where a manager falls in these dimensions significantly influences his perspective on a problem, a group, and his own abilities (Table 4).

Table 4. The six dimensions of cultural diversity

1	**Universalism.** Rules, codes, laws, and generalizations	**Particularism.** Exceptions, special circumstances, unique relations.
2	**Individualism.** Personal freedom, human rights, competitiveness.	**Communitarianism.** Social responsibility, harmonious relations, cooperation.
3	**Specificity.** Atomistic, reductive, analytic, objective.	**Diffusion.** Holistic, elaborative, synthetic, relational.
4	**Achieved Status.** What you've done, your track record.	**Ascribed Status.** Who you are, your potential, and connections.
5	**Inner Direction.** Conscience and convictions are located inside.	**Outer Direction.** Examples and influences are located outside.
6	**Sequential Time.** Time is a race along a set course.	**Synchronous Time.** Time is a dance of fine coordination.

Source: Hampton-Turner and Trompenaars, 2000

Jennings and Wattman (1998) also identify four different company cultures that influence decision making within organizations. These are:

- **Power Culture** in which power is concentrated within a single person or a small group. This is typical of a family owned business.
- **Role Culture** in which there is a very formal organization and the emphasis is on the role associated with each position, rather than the individual who occupies the position.
- **Task Culture** in which teams of employees work together on particular tasks. These teams often transcend a formal organizational structure.
- **Person Culture** in which the organization exists for the needs of its members, such as a commune or support group.

Both of these sources emphasize the fact that culture plays an important role in the style of decision making employed by individuals and groups.

Contributions of Models and Tools

Many of the decision making theories or processes investigated in this chapter are accompanied by models, tools, or simulations that capture the method and apply it in a systematic way. These tools are meant to augment human reasoning, understanding, and communication. As revealed, there are a number of limitations or constraints on a human individual or group's ability to make effective decisions. Daim (2006) lists three of these as:

1. Applying an open loop and linear approach to understanding a problem,
2. Ignoring the effect of feedback, and
3. Ignoring the effect of delayed consequences to our actions.

Some authors researched above, have prescribed a more objective perspective on information and actions to overcome this. However, many of them do not provide methods or tools to achieve this objectivism. Models and tools usually provide three major contributions to the decision making process:

1. *Perfect Memory*—Computer-based tools and structured written records capture and organize information such that it can be more effectively evaluated.

2. *Dynamic Representation*—Models can represent both the static state and the dynamic behavior of a system. Humans are particularly weak in predicting the dynamic behavior of a system.

- *Visualization*—Through numerous data presentation forms, models can present information in a way that can be understood by a wide variety of people. Abstract concepts can be made more concrete through visualization.

System dynamics models have been very visible and aggressive in promoting their ability to improve problem solving and decision making. Their abilities to bring out hidden cause-and-effect relationships and to illustrate the long term behavior of a system have won them many supporters. Stave (2002) quotes Jay Forrester as pointing out that these models are most valuable when they create "insight through surprise." In many cases, models simply quantify, visualize, and confirm behaviors that were already known. Their real value is when they can uncover a behavior or property of a system that is unsuspected and surprising in its nature.

System dynamics, statistics, decision trees, simulations, and computer games all make promises to revolutionize some aspect of business and decision making. Each usually makes a contribution, but seldom emerges as the Rosetta's Stone for decoding the intricacies of all problems. Figure 15.14 provides a conceptual map of a decision making process that includes teams of people. The core process can be augmented by models, simulations, and games in at least three stages—analysis, illustration, and prototyping. However, with or without these tools, the decision to take action remains a part of the human "leaderspace".

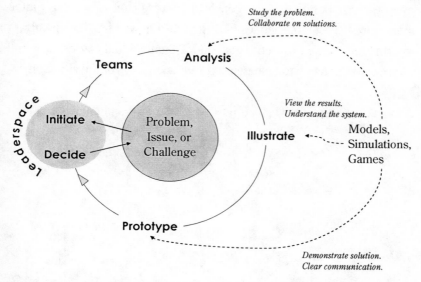

Figure 15.14 Decision making cycle and team problem analysis augmented by models, simulations, and game tools.

The quantitative nature of computer-based tools is their strength for memory, representation, and visualization. However, it can also be a weakness that misleads the decision making process. Homer (2001) points out that all models contain a number of uncertainties. However, computers demand objective definition in order to operate, so the degree of these uncertainties is often masked by the convincing definiteness of the tools. It is important for decision makers to understand the foundations upon which these tools reside to be able to appropriately discount the accuracy of their results.

Figure 15.15 inserts one emerging type of tool; computer games, into a decision making model to illustrate how it contributes to and changes the model. Games embody the mental models that are used by people, but make them more consistent across runs. They draw information from past experiences and existing knowledge. The insight or information created from the game adds to individual competence and may cause the users to change their mental models of the situation.

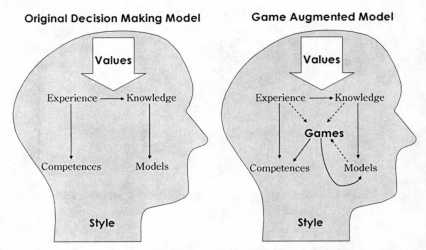

Games create a laboratory for testing existing models of decision making with prior knowledge and experience. This results in competence that is created from working with the game rather than pure experience. Experimentation with the game can also modify the models that are used in decision making.

Figure 15.15 Impact of game tools on the decision making process.

Models, tools, and games can all be used to improve decision making processes by:

1. *Replacing* mental processes that are inefficient,
2. *Extending* processes that are stretched to their limit by the size and complexity of a large problem, and
3. *Exploring* new problem spaces or dimensions that are beyond existing mental facilities or models.

Conclusion

In this chapter, we have explored a number of approaches to decision making, tools that are used to enhance the process, and the effects of the environment in which decisions are made. Decision making is a huge domain and is the predecessor to most actions. Small decisions seem to have very little decision making preceding them, but perhaps they simply have a very efficient method that reaches a conclusion quickly. Following Simon's bounded rationality theory, the amount of consideration that goes into a decision is never complete, but is scaled according to the importance of the consequences. Small daily actions include a rapid decision method that invests time and energy that is appropriate for the size of the action to be taken. Malcolm Gladwell's popular book, *Blink*, attempts to validate instant decision making by pointing to the accuracy of many intuitive or "gut" decisions and emphasizing that people possess internal maps of knowledge that are not necessarily understood, but remain relatively accurate (Gladwell 2005).

At the other extreme, major business decisions which involve large amounts of money, impact many people, and play out over long periods of time, demand a more rigorous and methodical decision making process. For these, statistical methods, expert systems, system dynamics, vigilant problem solving, the OODA loop, and real options can all be essential methods for optimizing a solution.

This chapter has exposed a number of major theories and processes for decision making. As each has come to light, the similarities with other methods become apparent. Mintzberg's generalized decision making model is certainly a good framework for many of these methods, and can be augmented with specialized steps and detailed analyses for each problem.

16

REAL OPTIONS THEORIES FOR RESEARCH PROJECT INVESTMENTS

In 1973, Fischer Black and Myron Scholes published their now fa-mous paper on an appropriate method to price financial options. This was later modified by Robert Merton and is sometimes referred to as the Black/Scholes/Merton (BSM) equation, or just the Black–Scho-les equation (Mandelbrot & Hudson, 2004). Their work extended the ideas of calculating the discounted cash flow (DCF) of a future asset, by including a measure of the uncertainty of future investments. This uncertainty represents opportunity that is not taken into account in a DCF equation. When this is applied to stocks and commodities op-tions, there is a huge database of information on the historical perfor-mance of assets that can be used to estimate future uncertainty levels, and derive an accurate measure of the future value of the option.

Once exposed to this concept, management consultants began to explore the application of real options to business decisions of all types. If the appropriate data could be collected or estimated, it may be possi-ble to calculate the value of a non-financial decision. Examples of these decisions include whether or not to invest in a new R&D concept or to open a new oil-drilling platform. Though the action will lead to financial investment and reward, the outcome of the decision is unknowable and non-deterministic. This makes it very difficult to apply both DCF and BSM equations to such problems.

Technology executives find themselves facing a wide array of deci-sions, such as monitoring and evaluating new technologies, contrib-uting to merger and acquisition decisions, selecting R&D projects to fund, identifying strategic directions for the company's technical capa-bilities, building the company's reputation with the media and govern-ment organizations, and championing the internal culture of innovation (Smith, 2003). Several of these activities can be cast as a real options valuation (ROV) problem and the BSM concepts may be applied. Decisions on which R&D projects to pursue are almost purely an options problem (Van Putten & MacMillan, 2004). In these cases, the company is investing in technologies before they are ready to become revenue-generating products. The investment is small in comparison to production costs, and is designed to equip the company with an understanding of the technology, the market, and the infrastructure necessary to create valuable products. In each case, the company will reach a position in which it must decide that the R&D option is "in-the-money" and should be exercised by going into production, or is "out-of-the-money" and should be terminated. R&D investment positions the company to capture future revenues, but still allows them to abandon the option investment if it will not become profitable.

Black/Scholes/Merton Options Valuation

McKinsey consultants, Keith Leslie and Max Michaels, have identified six levers on financial options value within the BSM equation (Leslie & Michaels, 2000). They attempt to convert these levers into comparable terms that can guide real option decisions. The BSM equation presents the value of an option (OV) as:

$$OV = Se^{-\partial t} * \{N(d_1)\} - Xe^{-rt} * \{N(d_2)\},$$
$$where, d_1 = \{\ln(S/X) + (r - \partial + \sigma^2/2)t\}/\sigma * \sqrt{t}$$
$$and, d_2 = d_1 - \sigma * \sqrt{t}$$

Where,

OV = Option Value

S = stock price,

X = exercise price,

δ = dividends,

r = risk-free rate,

σ = uncertainty (standard deviation),

t = time to expiry, and

N(d) = cumulative normal distribution value of 'd' where X is the mean and σ is the standard deviation.

Within this equation, there are six variables that influence the value of the option and determine whether it should be purchased. These are the stock price (S), exercise price (X), dividends (δ), risk-free rate (r), uncertainty (σ), and time to expiry (t). Several of these represent levers that are straightforward in real options situations as well. Leslie and Michaels use a hexagon to illustrate the similarities between the variables in a financial option and those in a real option (Figure 16.1). The exercise price, risk-free rate, and time to expiry, apply in both situations. Stock price is the hoped for end reward, though in the case of a real option, it is estimated. The two variables that are difficult to convert, are the measure of uncertainty and the dividends. Dividends represent the value that flows out of the stock price between the purchase of the option and its exercise (this is the modification to Black-Scholes that was added by Merton). Therefore, the dividend term of BSM is replaced with any event that would generate lost value on the real investment. A real example of this may be the discovery of a new compound by a university lab and the release of that information into the public domain. If this compound had been discovered within the company labs, the information would have remained a secret and become part of the IP of the company, rather than being lost to the public domain. The release of that information into the public domain is like the loss of a dividend on an optioned stock. This leaves us in an uncertain position about uncertainty. When dealing with equities, historical data on stock performance can be used to calculate a standard deviation on the price. This becomes the measure of uncertainty for the asset. However, with real options, there is much less information from which to work and some other method must be used. Van Putten suggests an approach to this issue that we will explore in a later section.

The six levers of financial and real options

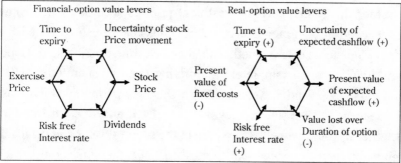

Figure 16.1 Financial options use six variables to calculate value. Real options take advantage f this equation by making subtle changes to the meaning of those six variables. *(Leslie, 2000)*

Real Decision-making

Successful managers have long exercised caution in making decisions about major investments or changes in strategy. In an effort to find the best path, they have used prototypes, experiments, research, surveys, and consultants. Each of these is a tool to gain knowledge before making a decision. Each is an investment designed to reduce the probability (or risk) of making the wrong choice. In this sense, each of these is a learning option (Amram & Kulatilake, 1999). Following an investment and/or the passage of time, the manager can apply new knowledge in a decision to abstain from further investment, or to move forward and invest in the project. The money invested in the prototype, experiment, or consultant is the price of this option.

However, since this is a real option, the option price does not really guarantee the acquisition of an asset at a predetermined price. Rather, it reduces risk and illuminates the future in an attempt to determine whether the estimated full investment price is accurate. Once some measure of its accuracy is attained, it is possible to use DCF or ROV techniques to calculate whether further investment is justified. Copeland provides one example of the differing results generated by DCF and ROV (Copeland & Keenan, 1998). During a period in which most PC makers were losing money, he used DCF and ROV to estimate whether it would be better for some of the money-losing companies to remain in the business or exit (Figure 16.2). DCF suggested that they should exit unless they could achieve gross operating margins of 13% or better. However, ROV suggested that they should stay in with operating margins as low as 9%, because of the high volatility in the industry and the large long-term profits that were possible. This is a simple illustration of the different projections that come from the two methods.

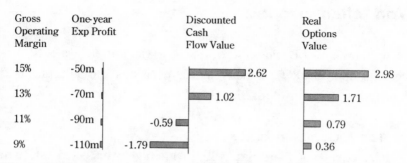

Gross Operating Margin	One-year Exp Profit		Discounted Cash Flow Value		Real Options Value
15%	-50m			2.62	2.98
13%	-70m			1.02	1.71
11%	-90m		-0.59		0.79
9%	-110m	-1.79			0.36

Figure 16.2 Copeland illustrated the significant differences in value that can be generated by DCF and ROV. In this example, ROV suggests that the value of the PC business is positive with margins as low as 9%, while DCF suggests that 13% margins are necessary to generate positive value. *(Copeland, 1997)*

Van Putten wrestles with the issue of the difference between what an option buys you in financial decisions and what it buys in non-financial decisions (Van Putten & MacMillan, 2004). He recognized that DCF and ROV both apply to very restricted financial situations, and that real decisions come with fewer constraints; hence, less certainty.

BSM treats uncertainty as equally distributed around a mean. This may be an accurate representation for financial products, but is not characteristic of real projects. Van Putten points out that project costs seldom vary as much below the budgeted/average value as they do above. It is common to hear of a $200 million project that overshot its budget by 50%, and is expected to be completed for $300 million. However, it is almost unheard of for that project to come in 50% under its budget at $100 million. BSM treats both of these variations as equally likely. Therefore, van Putten suggests that a pure BSM approach to real options valuation (ROV) is not a good idea. Rather, it should be combined with a DCF approach. Even then, there are situations in which the ROV needs to be adjusted to more appropriately address the real world.

Van Putten's Process

In his Harvard Business Review article, van Putten lays out a process for applying ROV to non-financial decisions and adjusting it to more accurately reflect real decisions.

Step 1. Combine ROV & DCF

ROV equations, like BSM, will provide higher expected values to investments when uncertainty is high, and this number will decrease as uncertainty decreases. In most cases, the primary driver that decreases uncertainty is the flow of time. Therefore, when an option is far out in time, the ROV will assign a high value to the option. DCF, on the other hand, will generate smaller numbers in this situation because it is driven by the time-value of money. Therefore, van Putten suggests that at this extreme edge, the results of an ROV calculation should be balanced against a more conservative DCF. If DCF suggests that the value is significantly negative, then decision-makers should discount the ROV results and decide not to make the investment in spite of the positive ROV numbers. This is what he calls the "Flee Zone" in Figure 16.3.

Managers can rely on a mathematically combined ROV and DCF equation as the option date gets closer to the exercise date. As time decreases, the impact of DCF increases and the results of combining the two become more directly useful.

Finally, when the time becomes very near the exercise date, the ROV contributes very little to the value, because uncertainty has almost completely disappeared. In this case, when a positive value is achieved, the ROV is "Deep-in-the-Money", uncertainty is at a minimum, and managers are making decisions almost completely based on DCF.

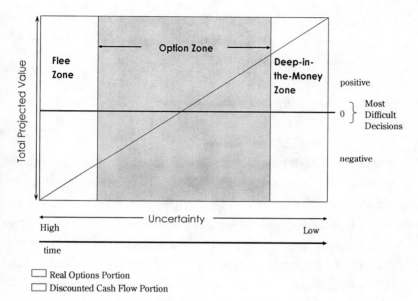

☐ Real Options Portion
☐ Discounted Cash Flow Portion

Figure 16.3 van Putten presented a method for combining ROV and DCF in determining the expected value of a project. This method gives more emphasis to DCF when the end of the project is near, but more to ROV when the time is longer and uncertainty is higher. *(van Putten, 2004)*

Step 2. Adjust ROV

In the second step, van Putten points out that ROV places equal value on variations in revenue and costs. Revenues may vary greatly above and below the mean prediction. However, costs are much more likely to vary upward than downward. Therefore, the ROV number should be adjusted to account for this. When cost volatility exceeds revenue volatility, then the overall project volatility should be adjusted by the ratio of revenue to cost volatility.

adjusted volatility = project volatility x (revenue vol / cost vol)

Conversely, when cost volatility does not exceed revenue volatility, then the adjusted volatility value should be set to 1. This leads to the option's Adjusted Option Value (AOV).

AOV = ROV * adjusted volatility

Step 3. Abandonment value

Real options are different from financial options, in that there is a residual value even if the company decides not to exercise the option. In financial markets, the decision not to exercise completely eliminates the asset that was optioned. However, in the real world, the results of the option investment may be a residual technology, laboratory facilities and equipment, intellectual property, etc. This residual has value and should be included in the calculation of the option value, if an estimate of its value can be made. Van Putten suggests that whenever possible, managers should strive to bring this "abandonment value" into existence. This may be accomplished by agreeing to license or sell the residual results, like IP, to a partner if the host company decides not to proceed with the project.

Option Value Calculation

Applying all of these steps, van Putten suggests that the value of a real option should be calculated as:

TPV = NPV + AOV + ABV

Where,

TPV = total project value
NPV = net present value
AOV = adjusted option value (steps 1 & 2)
ABV = abandonment value (step 3)

Finally, since ROV is being applied to a real-world problem where the variables impacting outcomes are not bounded as tightly as they are in the financial markets, it is impossible for an equation to accurately predict future outcomes. Therefore, the ROV methods are useful in providing quantitative measures of multiple projects. Van Putten points out that most businesses have a large number of project options from which to choose. The Adjusted ROV can be helpful in ranking these for comparison. However, it should not be trusted as an absolute measure of the financial outcome of a real decision.

Real Options Thinking

Given the perspective of the authors referenced, it is clear that real options analysis is different from cautious business decision-making. The key difference is in the analytical mindset that forces a manager to quantify information that was previously evaluated in a very intuitive way. This is particularly valuable when applying the method to multiple projects that will be compared with each other. It assists in minimizing subjective biases for or against a project; placing them all on a more even footing when competing for funding.

Disadvantages that may arise include slowing decisions down in order to gather quantitative data to calculate ROV or AOV. When data is difficult to get, it can make this process more of a hindrance than help. It may also empower "bean counters" with tools that can overthrow the judgment of more experienced leaders. To some degree, this is the goal of quantification, but it is not intended as a replacement for experience and wisdom.

Example of the Combination of ROV, NPV, and Abandonment Value

The ideas presented in this article and in the referenced papers can be difficult to implement numerically. Therefore, we have created a Microsoft Excel spreadsheet that performs these calculations based on the required inputs. That spreadsheet implements van Putten's ideas for real options by calculating the Total Project Value by combining Real Options Value, Adjusted Options Value, Net Present Value, and Abandonment Value, using the equations listed here.

Real Option Value:

$$ROV = Se^{-\partial t} * \{N(d_1)\} - Xe^{-rt} * \{N(d_2)\},$$
$$where, d_1 = \{\ln(S/X) + (r - \partial + \sigma^2/2)t\}/\sigma * \sqrt{t}$$
$$and, d_2 = d_1 - \sigma * \sqrt{t}$$

where,

ROV = Option Value

S = Present value of expected cashflow,

X = Present value of fixed costs,

δ = Value lost over duration of option,

r = risk-free interest rate,

σ = Uncertainty of expected cashflow (standard deviation),

t = time to expiry, and

N(d) = cumulative normal distribution function.

Adjusted Option Value:

$$AOV = AV * ROV$$
$$AV = PV * \left[\frac{RV}{CV}\right]$$

where,

AOV = Adjusted Option Volatility

AV = Adjustment to Volatility

If CV < RV, the AV=1

PV = Project Volatility

RV = Revenue Volatility

CV = Cost Volatility

Net Present Value:

$$NPV = \sum_{t=0}^{N} \frac{C_t}{(1+i)^t} - X$$

Where,

NPV = Net Present Value

t = time period

C_t = Investment during time period t

N = number of periods to recoup investment

i = risk free interest rate

X = Initial Investment

Abandonment Value:

ABV = Residual value of investment in the project at completion

Total Project Value:

TPV = NPV + AOV + ABV

The table provides the estimated value of a small R&D project using the spreadsheet. In this case, the NPV was positive and the ROV and AOV were negative. However, the predominant value of the project after five years was in the value of the residual equipment and IP that existed after the project was completed. This led to a Total Project Value that was much higher than either the NPV or the ROV alone.

TPV	$26,318						
ROV	-$7	AOV	-$3	NPV	$6,321	ABV	$20,000
S	$100,000	AV	39.29%	N	5		
X	$10,000	PV	50%	I	5%		
δ	$20,000	RV	55%	X	$10,000		
r	5%	CV	70%	Ct(0)	$0		
σ	$50,000			Ct(1)			
t	5			Ct(2)			
				Ct(3)	$10,000		
				Ct(4)			
				Ct(5)			

17

R&D PRODUCTIVITY

Japan, Western Europe, and the United States, are facing challenges to their dominance of the world economy. Countries like India, China, and those in Eastern Europe are developing manufacturing and service capabilities that offer competent and lower priced alternatives (Christensen, 1997). To counter this, established countries are turning to technology and legal barriers to defend their positions, and to carry them into positions that are less vulnerable to competition. Technology is created through investments in research and development (R&D). Legal barriers are created through patents on new technology, processes, and other intellectual property (Christensen & Raynor, 2003).

The amount of money invested in R&D, is one measure of the degree to which US countries are moving to new products and services that cannot be matched by upstart countries (Gonzalez & Pazo, 2004). Many researchers are conducting studies to try to determine the degree to which R&D really improves a company's performance (Bae & Kim, 2003; Chauvin & Hirschey, 1993; Youndt et al, 2004; Szewczyk et al, 1996). In this study, I examined published data on the level of R&D investment made by US companies. The goal was to identify a relationship between R&D spending (the dependent variable) and other financial indicators of the company's health (the independent variables). Such a model, and the understanding that accompanies it, will be useful in predicting how companies may invest in the future, and at what levels a company might fund new R&D capabilities. Models were sought which could predict future year spending based on previous year financials; but also models which demonstrated a relationship between current year R&D and current year financials. The latter model would not have predictive power, but would be useful in identifying when a company's R&D investment is out of line with other companies among the top investors in R&D.

This study was conducted to determine whether there is any correlation between the amount of money that a company invests in research and development (R&D) and other financial and employment statistics. Previous studies have shown that R&D intensity (R&D divided by Sales) is consistent within a company from one year to another. This statistic is one method of estimating the level of R&D that a company will invest in future years. However, R&D investment may be more complicated than that. It may be driven by a combination of quantitative factors, which is the focus of this study. It should also be noted, that R&D investment is a strategic decision and may change greatly based on the objectives of the company. When major changes occur from one year to another, these cannot be captured in a general quantitative model as presented in this paper.

This study and data analysis provides a more complete understanding of the data presented in IRI's annual R&D Leaderboard surveys. It provides a predictive tool for understanding the actions of R&D investors. This type of understanding and predictive power is not evident in the raw data that is published in the annual survey.

The study focuses on 91 companies that appeared in the list of the Top 100 U.S. R&D investors for both 2003 and 2004. Each year, a few companies are displaced from this Top 100 list. In 2004, nine companies were displaced, which led to the size of the sample data used in this study.

Limitations of the Study

This study contains two limitations that should be clearly acknowledged. First, it was conducted across the top R&D investing firms in the United States. Therefore, the R&D investment data is a view into only medium and large-sized companies. The largest company by sales in this list is Exxon Mobile with 2004 sales of $264 billion. The smallest company is Synopsys with sales of $1.09 billion (Whitley, 2005). Therefore, the results of this study may not be applicable to smaller companies that have fewer resources or where innovation is applied on a smaller scale. Second, the firms were all based in the United States. Though many of them have international operations, these companies are American in their legal structure, in the heritage of their management thinking, and in their approach to business. Therefore, the information discovered will be characteristic of U.S. companies and may not capture practices that are common in other parts of the world.

The conclusions and models in this study can be extended by applying the methodology to a larger database of companies that reside in both the U.S. and around the world. Such a study may be carried out by organizations with access to larger sets of R&D investment data.

Data Set Analyzed

This study was based on annual R&D Leaderboard data that is published in Research Technology Management. Those papers identify the companies that invest the most in R&D each year. The data is usually organized into four tables that identify the top 100 US companies, top 1,000 US companies, top 100 global companies, and top 1,000 global companies. Both of the "Top 100" tables are published in the Research Technology Management journal. The "Top 1,000" tables are available for purchase from the Industrial Research Institute.

The data presented in these surveys is extracted from the Standard & Poor's COMPUSTAT database. For over 35 years, Standard & Poor's has maintained the COMPUSTAT database of company operations data. It contains records on over 10,000 actively traded U.S. companies, 11,000 inactive U.S. companies, 1,100 Canadian companies, and an unspecified number of International companies. COMPUSTAT contains organizational and operating information on each company as well as data on aggregate industry sectors (S&P, 2005).

The data that was used for this study did not come from a designed experiment. It is observational data that was collected from multiple companies at specific points in time. This means that there are many external forces on company activities that are not controlled for in the data. In such a situation, it is very difficult to draw cause-and-effect conclusions about any relationships identified in the data. We are limited to identifying a correlation between variables and are not in a position to state that one variable causes specific changes in another. We are able to predict the behavior of one variable from that of others, but cannot state that one causes a specific quantifiable change in the other.

The R&D Leaderboard data includes a number of variables beyond investment in R&D. These variables are described in Table 1. For this study, I used financial data reported by the companies for their fiscal years 2004, 2003, and 2002

Table 1. R&D Leaderboard variables available for inclusion
in the regression model.

Variable	Definition
Name of Company	Name of the company
Ranking of Company	Ranking among the Top 100 in both 2003 and in 2004.
R&D Investment	Millions of dollars invested in R&D in the years 2003 and 2004.
Annual Change in R&D investment	Percentage change in R&D investment from 2003 to 2004, and from 2002 to 2003.
R&D Investment per 1,000 Employees	R&D investment divided by thousands of employees in the company during the given year.
R&D as a Percentage of Sales	R&D divided by sales to determine its percentage with respect to sales.
R&D as a percentage of Profits	R&D divided by profits.
Annual Sales	Millions of dollars in gross sales in the years 2003 and 2004.
Annual Change in Sales	Percentage change in sales from 2003 to 2004, and from 2002 to 2003.
Sales per 1,000 Employees	Annual sales divided by the number of employees in thousands.
Annual Profits	Annual after-tax profits of the company in millions of dollars.
Annual Change in Profit	Percentage change in profits from 2003 to 2004, and from 2002 to 2003.
Profits as a Percentage of Sales	Profits divided by sales.
Capital Expenses	Amount spent on capital during the year in millions of dollars.
Capital Expenses as a Percentage of Sales	Capital expenses divided by sales for the year.

All financial data is presented in millions of US dollars in these tables.

In this study, I created and validated two equations capable of predicting the amount of money that a company will invest in R&D in a given year. Using the information provided, I constructed two regression equations with a dependent variable of R&D investment for 2004. The independent variables for the model are extracted from the list provided in Table 1. These variables include values for the current and the previous years.

Building a Linear Model

I took several distinct steps in modeling this data. Because there was no previous knowledge of relationships within the data, and because the goal was to identify any correlations with the independent variables, I conducted a number of tests to explore the wide variety of relationships that might exist. The process of building the model is described in this section, along with some embedded model analysis. More in-depth analyses were conducted on the models but are not included as part of this paper.

Scatter Plot Data

The first step was to plot pairs of variables from the table. These plots are two-dimensional Cartesian scatter-plots of one independent variable and one dependent variable. These were an important first step in visually revealing simple relationships within the data. They created an initial understanding of the data to guide the model building process. Each of the plots that follow includes the names of some of the companies that bound the edges of the data.

The first set of plots (Figures 17.1, 17.2, and 17.3), compare current year R&D spending to previous year spending. These demonstrate a very strong linear relationship between these variables. I was quite surprised to discover such a strong relationship. These graphs suggest that current year R&D spending can be very accurately predicted from the previous year's R&D spending. The plots that compare adjacent years show a much higher degree of correlation than does the plot comparing 2004 data to that from 2002.

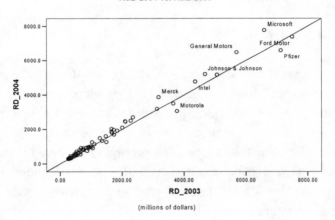

Figure 17.1 Current year (2004) R&D spending is highly correlated with previous year (2003) R&D spending. The correlation between consecutive years, is stronger than between any other pairs of variables investigated.

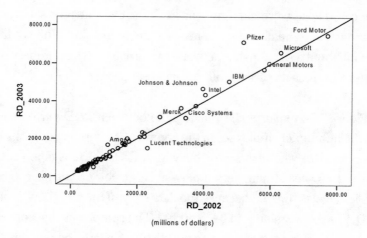

Figure 17.2 The correlation between 2003 and 2002 R&D spending, is nearly as strong as that for 2004 and 2003.

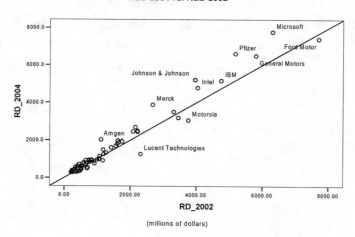

Figure 17.3 Correlation between 2004 and 2002 R&D spending begins to diverge, indicating that R&D spending is not a constant from one year to the next.

Additional graphs explored the relationships between current year finances. These were current year R&D vs. current year sales; R&D vs. profits, and the change in sales vs. change in R&D. None of these demonstrated a relationship between the variables. The numbers were scattered across the graph with no apparent pattern.

Figure 17.4 explores the relationship between R&D per employee and the number of employees in the company. This indicates that smaller companies, who also invest heavily in R&D, have a much higher level of R&D investment per employee. Large companies have a much smaller level. However, because the data set is of the top 91 investors in R&D, this relationship is to be expected. The companies that appear on this list tend to be of two varieties. First, the very large companies such as Exxon Mobil, GE, GM, IBM, and Ford who have very high sales and that perform very broad sets of activities. Because these companies are large, they must have a large number of employees who have nothing to do with technology or research; leading to a low ratio of R&D per employee. Second are high technology companies that have to invest in R&D in order to remain competitive. This includes companies in biotechnology, medicine, and computers.

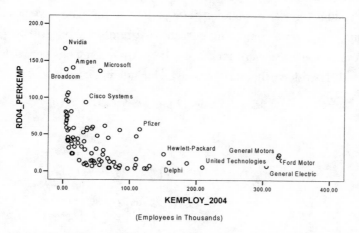

R&D Per 1000 Employees

(Employees in Thousands)

Figure 17.4 Levels of R&D investment are not strongly correlated with the number of employees. Though larger companies tend to invest more in R&D, the increase is not proportional to employment numbers.

All of these graphs were created to assist in identifying significant variables to be considered in creating regression models for R&D spending. I used this information to guide the selection of independent variables to include in the stepwise linear analysis.

One Year Offset

The list of independent variables included sales, profit, and R&D numbers from previous years, as well as the current year. It is possible that R&D spending is driven primarily by previous years' sales and profits, and is not as strongly correlated to those of the current year. Working from the data sets given in Whiteley (2005) and Armbrecht and Whiteley (2004), I can identify previous year data for 2003 and 2002 for the 91 companies included in the study.

Figure 17.5 compares previous year changes in sales with current year changes in R&D spending. The pattern in the data is very similar to that found when comparing current year numbers, but with perhaps a stronger leaning toward increasing R&D when previous year sales increased. Therefore, this variable will be included in later model building.

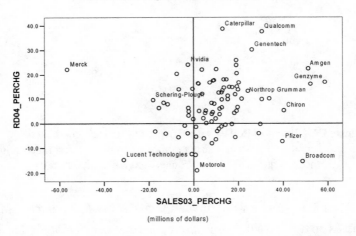

Figure 17.5. Increases in current year R&D are generally aligned with previous year increases in sales. However, it appears that many companies are setting their R&D based on factors other than simple correlation with previous year increases in sales.

Algorithms were also created which explored the relationships between 2004 R&D spending and 2003 sales and profits. No statistical relationship was evident between these variables.

The graphs provided in these two sections were intended to reveal simple relationships between two variables. In the case of current and previous year R&D, an extremely strong relationship is very evident. This played an important role in the model building that follows.

Qualitative Variables and Piecewise Linear Regression

Some variables may be better represented as qualitative variables. The plots may indicate specific breakpoints in the relationships between the dependent and independent variables. For example, the size of the company may be well represented by qualitative variables that indicate whether the company is small, medium, or large. This type of relationship may also exist for the level of capital investment used by a company. Companies may be best represented as heavy or light users of capital investment, rather than representing the quantitative value of the investment.

To explore these relationships, I created three qualitative variables. One identifies companies that have 2004 sales of more than $50 billion (large). Another identifies companies that have 2004 sales of less than $1 billion (small). These are used to separate companies into small, medium, and large categories.

I also created a qualitative variable to identify companies with 2004 capital expenditures of more than $1 billion (high).

These three variables introduce a piecewise linear relationship into the model. The first two are functions of 2004 sales, and the third is a function of 2004 capital expenditure; both of which are included in one of the models.

Stepwise Regression Analysis

Rather than manually creating and testing a number of regression models from the variables described above; I used the stepwise regression functions found in the SPSS statistical analysis software package to automatically conduct the many replications necessary to identify the best fitting combinations of independent variables. The stepwise regression tool identifies the set of variables that best fit the data and indicates the level of fit to that data for a progressive list of possible models. This removes much of the manual work involved in creating models, but still provides a clear understanding of the level of fit that can be achieved from a number of different models.

R&D Investment Based on Sales, Profits, and Capital

The first model correlates current year R&D spending using current and previous year sales, profits, and capital expenditures as independent variables. The SPSS stepwise modeling tool generated the following model as the best fit using these variables,

$$y_s = 420.812 - .403\, x_1 + .621\, x_2 + .455\, x_3 - .456\, x_4 - 1768.376\, x_5 + 1054.801\, x_6$$

where,

y_s = 2004 R&D Investments

x_1 = 2004 Sales

x_2 = 2004 Profits

x_3 = 2003 Sales

x_4 = 2003 Profits

x_5 = Large Company (qualitative) = 1 if 2004 Sales (x_1) >= $50 billion, 0 otherwise

x_6 = Large Capital (qualitative) = 1 if 2004 Capital Expenditure > $1 billion, 0 otherwise

R^2 is 73.8% and $R_{(adj)}^2$ is 72.0%.

The R^2 and $R_{(adj)}^2$ values are measures of the degree to which this model accounts for the variation that exists in the original data. Though 72% is a good level of correlation with the data, the selection of independent variables creates a limitation to its use. Because it requires knowledge of current year sales and profits, it cannot be used to predict future R&D investments for a company. I examined a number of other models that did not use current year financials as independent variables. Unfortunately, those yielded correlation levels of less than 40%, making them poor predictors of R&D spending.

R&D Investment Based on Previous Year R&D

The simple plots of current year versus previous year R&D that were presented above indicate that there is a very strong correlation between these numbers. Therefore, I used the SPSS stepwise regression tool to explore a model in which R&D investments in 2003 and 2002 are used to predict 2004 R&D investment levels. This analysis led to the following model,

$$y_r = 17.274 + 1.033\, x_1 - 211.830\, x_2 + 186.96\, x_3$$

where,

y_r = 2004 R&D Investments

x_1 = 2003 R&D Investments

x_2 = Large Company (qualitative) = 1 if 2004 Sales (x_1) >= $50 billion, 0 otherwise

x_3 = Large Capital (qualitative) = 1 if 2004 Capital Expenditure > $1 billion, 0 otherwise

R^2 is 98.5% and $R_{(adj)}^2$ is 98.5%.

The degree of correlation for this model is extremely high at 98.5%, and requires many fewer variables than the first model created. However, the tool also identified a simpler model as being a very good fit to the data. A model that uses only the previous year R&D investment level to predict that of the current year achieved a correlation level of 98.3%. It is significantly simpler than the previous model and has a degree of fit that is only 0.2% lower than the more complex model. Because this model may be much more flexible when applied to international companies or to those outside of the Top 100, I believe it is a much more useful predictive tool.

$$y_r = 33.016 + 1.039\,x_1$$

where,

y_r = 2004 R&D Investments
x_1 = 2003 R&D Investments
R^2 is 98.3% and $R_{(adj)}^2$ is 98.3%.

The two models presented above can be useful under different circumstances. The first (designated y_s) can estimate current year R&D when other current and previous year financial data is available. The second (designated y_r) can predict current year R&D directly from R&D spending in the previous year, and no current year financial data.

Conclusion and Future Research

This analysis resulted in a pair of equations that can be used in comparing R&D investment across multiple companies, and in predicting what competitors are most likely to invest in the next year. Each model depends on different input values and may be useful under different conditions. In an attempt to illustrate the degree to which each model is able to match the R&D investment data from the original sources, I have constructed a scatterplot that includes three different data sets. Figure 17.6 shows three data sets overlaid on a single coordinate system. The independent variable (x-axis) for these is 2003 R&D investment in millions of dollars. The dependent variable (y-axis) is 2004 R&D investment.

On this graph, the circles represent the raw data that was originally presented in Whiteley (2005). The crosses plot the calculated 2004 R&D investment level using a model based on sales, profits, size, and capital (y_s, labeled PRED1 in the graph). This data has a 72.0% correlation with the actual data. The triangles plot the calculated 2004 R&D investment level using the model based on 2003 R&D investment levels (y_r, labeled PRED2 in the graph). This data has a 98.3% correlation with the actual data.

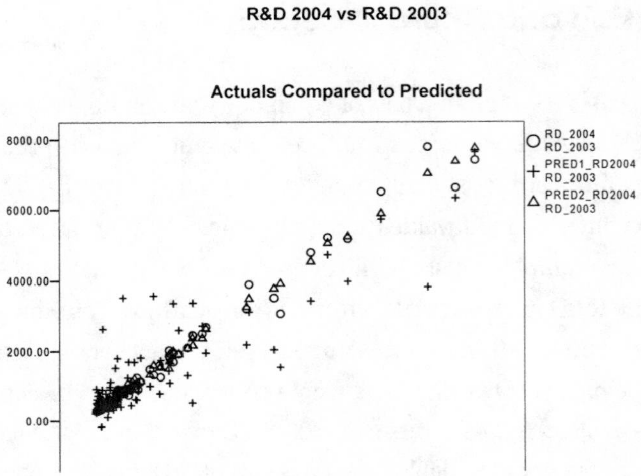

R&D 2004 vs R&D 2003

Actuals Compared to Predicted

Figure 17.6 This scatterplot illustrates the level of correlation between the actual R&D data and that generated by the two models created in this study. The "PRED2" model that is simply based on previous year R&D levels fits the data best for 2003 and 2004. The "PRED1" model includes more factors and may be more useful in a dynamic environment when sales vary more.

This study was limited to 91 of the Top 100 U.S. R&D investors in 2004. Therefore, the regression equations can only be applied reliably when company data falls into the ranges represented by these companies. However, this methodology can also be applied to a much larger set of corporate financial data to determine whether it can be applied much more broadly. It may also be applied to data on companies from outside of the United States to determine whether the model is characteristic of those.

Finally, I want to emphasize that the models in this paper can be used for planning within your own company, but they are also tools for analyzing and predicting the behavior of competitors. The models can be used to predict the R&D levels of an entire group of competitors in a consistent way. Once their actual R&D numbers are known, the variance with the predicted numbers may indicate that the competitor has incorporated some new strategy into the R&D investment.

These models are just one tool in the internal R&D planning and competitive analysis process. They should be combined with other techniques to arrive at optimal decisions.

Appendix A: Companies Analyzed

This appendix provides a complete list of the 91 companies that were included in this study. This is a subset of the "Top 100" R&D investors from 2004 as presented Whiteley (2005), based on data available in Standard & Poor's COMPUSTAT database; as of July 31, 2005. Nine companies were omitted from the original "Top 100" list because they were new to the list in 2004, and data was not available for those companies for 2003 and 2002.

Microsoft	Lucent Technologies	Automatic Data Processing	Allergan
Ford Motor	United Technologies	Boston Scientific	Nvidia
Pfizer	3M	Broadcom	National Semiconductor
General Motors	Dow Chemical	Baxter International	General Dynamics
Johnson & Johnson	Applied Materials	Guidant	Maxtor
IBM	Freescale Semiconductor	Johnson Controls	Whirlpool
Intel	Lockheed Martin	Analog Devices	Lexmark Intl
Merck	Medtronic	Monsanto	Adobe Systems
Hewlett-Packard	Advanced Micro Devices	Northrop Grumman	Textron
Cisco Systems	Caterpillar	Agere Systems	Maxim Integrated Products
Motorola	Honeywell	Raytheon	PPG Industries
Eli Lilly	Agilent Tech	Apple Computer	Siebel Systems
Bristol-Myers Squibb	Visteon	Emerson Electric	Unisys
Wyeth	EMC Corp	Dell	Synopsys
General Electric	Eastman Kodak	Chiron	Amazon.com
Delphi	Genentech	LSI Logic	Intuit
Amgen	Altria Group	Genzyme	
Texas Instruments	Xerox	Kraft Foods	
Sun Microsystems	Micron Technology	Goodyear Tire & Rubber	
Boeing	Qualcomm	Appelera Consolidated	
Procter & Gamble	Computer Assoc	Autoliv	
Abbott Laboratories	Exxon Mobile	Cadence Design Systems	
Schering-Plough	ITT Industries	Corning	
Oracle	Electronic Arts	Avaya	
Du Pont	Deere & Co	Veritas Software	

Original Source: Whiteley, 2005

18

REFERENCES

Abt, C. (1970). *Serious games*. New York: The Viking Press.

Agricultural Development Initiatives. (2004). Biography of Rita Schnipke. http://www.agri-develop.org/rjs.html

Amram, M. & Kulatilaka, N. (February 1999). "Disciplined Decisions: Aligning Strategy with the Financial Markets". *Harvard Business Review*, 77(1), 95-104.

Argyris, C. (Mar-Apr 1966). "Interpersonal barriers to decision making". *Harvard Business Review*.

Armbrecht, F. & Whiteley, R. (January-February, 2002). "Industrial Research Institute's 3rd annual R&D leaderboard: R&D spending by the top 100 U.S. technology investors in 2000". *Research Technology Management*, 45(1), 21-23.

Armbrecht, F. & Whiteley, R. (January-February, 2003). "Industrial Research Institute's 4th annual R&D leaderboard: R&D spending by the top 100 U.S. technology investors in 2001". *Research Technology Management*, 46(1), 21-23.

Armbrecht, F. & Whiteley, R. (November-December, 2003). "Industrial Research Institute's 5th annual R&D leaderboard: R&D spending by the top 100 U.S. technology investors in 2002". *Research Technology Management*, 46(6), 19-23.

Armbrecht, F. & Whiteley, R. (November-December, 2004). "Industrial Research Institute's 6th annual R&D leaderboard: R&D spending by the top 100 U.S. technology investors in 2003". *Research Technology Management*, 47(6), 20-24.

Ashkanasy, N.; Windsor, C.; & Trevino, L. (Fall 2006). "Bad apples in bad barrels revisited: Cognitive moral development, just world beliefs, rewards, and ethical decision-making". Business Ethics Quarterly, 16(4).

Aspatore Editors. (2000). *Inside the Minds of Chief Technology Officers*. New York: Aspatore Books.

Bae, S. & Kim, D. (Winter, 2003). "The effect of R&D investments on market value of firms: Evidence from the U.S., Germany, and Japan". *Multinational Business Review*, 11(3), 51-75.

Baldwin, H. (January 26, 2004). "2004 InfoWorld CTO 25". *InfoWorld Magazine*. p.37-48.

Banks, J., ed. (1998). *Handbook of Simulation: Principles, methodology, advances, applications, and practice*. New York: John Wiley & Sons.

Barnard, C. (1938). *The Functions of the executive*. Cambridge, MA: Harvard University Press.

Bell, D. 1973. *The Coming of post-industrial society: A Venture in social forecasting*. New York: Basic Books.

Bennis, W. 1997. *Organizing genius: The Secrets of creative collaboration*. Reading, MA: Addison-Wesley.

Berry, G. (October 2006). "Can computer-mediated asynchronous communication improve team processes and decision making: Learning from the management literature". *Journal of Business Communications*, 43(4).

Betz, F. (1993). *Strategic Technology Management*. New York: McGraw Hill.

Bharadwaj, R. (January, 2002). The role of the CTO at Ejasent. Personal correspondence with the author.

Blue Ridge Numerics. (2004). Management Team. http://www.cfdesign.com/CompanyInfo/ExecutiveTeam.asp

Boyd, J. (June 1995). "The Essence of Winning and Losing". Address to Air University, Maxwell AFB, Alabama. Last presentation of John Boyd retrieved October 21, 2006 from http://www.belisarius.com/modern_business_strategy/boyd/essence/eowl_frameset.htm

Brewer, G. & Shubik, M. (1979). *The War game: A Critique of military problem solving*. Cambridge, MA: Harvard University Press.

Brigham, E. & Houston, J. (1999). *Fundamentals of financial management*. Fort Worth, Texas: Harcourt Brace.

Brunner, G.F. (January, 2001). "The Tao of innovation". *Research Technology Management*, 44(1), pp. 45-51.

Buderi, R. (2000). *Engines of Tomorrow: How the world's best companies are using their research labs to win the future*. New York: Simon & Schuster.

Buderi, R. June 2002. "Mhyrvold's exponential economy". *Technology Review* online.

http://www.technologyreview.com/articles/print_version/qa0602.asp

Burgelman, Robert A., Christensen, Clayton M. & Wheelwright, Steven C. 2004. *Strategic Management of Technology and Innovation*, (4th Ed.), Chicago, IL: Irwin Publishers.

Burke, L. & Miller, M. (November 1999). "Taking the mystery out of intuitive decision making". *Academy of Management Executive*, 13(4).

Burns, T. & Stalker, G.M. (1961). *Management of Innovation*. Oxford: Oxford University Press.

Carr, N.G. (2004). *Does IT Matter? Information Technology and the Corrosion of Competitive Advantage*. Boston: Harvard Business School Press.

Carr, N.G. (May 2003). "IT Doesn't Matter". *Harvard Business Review*. Boston: Harvard Business School Press.

Carr, N.G. (May 27, 2004). "The Z Curve and IT Investment". *Digital Renderings*. Nicholas G. Carr web site. http://www.nicholasgcarr.com/digital_renderings/archives/the_z_curve_and_it.shtml

Chakravorti, B. (2003). *The Slow pace of fast change: Bringing innovations to market in a connected world*. Boston, MA: Harvard Business School Press.

Chandler, A. 2001. *Inventing the electronic century: The Epic story of the consumer electronics and computer industries*. New York: Free Press.

Chauvin, K. & Hirschey, M. (Winter 1993). "Advertising, R&D expenditures and the market value of the firm". *Financial Management*, 22(1), 128-140.

Chesbrough, Henry. (2003). *Open Innovation: The New Imperative for Creating and Profiting from Technology*. Harvard Business School Press.

Christensen, C. & Raynor, M. (2003). *The Innovator's solution: Creating and sustaining successful growth*. Boston: Harvard Business School Press.

Christensen, C. (1997). *The Innovator's dilemma: When new technologies cause great firms to fail*. Boston, MA: Harvard Business School Press.

Christensen, C. (1999). *Innovation and the General Manager*, Boston, MA: Irwin McGraw-Hill.

Christensen, C. & Overdorf, M. (March-April 2000). "Meeting the challenge of disruptive change". *Harvard Business Review*.

Christensen, C. & Raynor, M. (2003). *The Innovators solution: Creating and sustaining successful growth*. Boston, MA: Harvard Business School Press.

City of Cleveland. (2004). Biography of Melody Mayberry-Stewart. http://www.city.cleveland.oh.us/government/cabinet/biographies/mayberrystewart.html

Clarck, S. (December 22, 2003). "City Picks Telecom Winner". CrainTech. http://www.onecleveland.org/NE%20Ohio%20CrainTech%2012-22-03.htm

Colborn, K. & Peterson, P. (December 2002). "Dawn Meyerriecks is CTO of DISA", Diversity/Careers. http://www.diversitycareers.com/articles/pro/decjan03/att_meyerriecks.htm

Copeland, T.E., & Keenan, P.T. (1998). "How much is flexibility worth?" *The McKinsey Quarterly*, 2, 38-50.

Council on Competitiveness. (December 2004). "Innovate America: National Innovation Initiative Report—thriving in a world of challenge and change". U.S. Council on Competitiveness.

Cusumano, M. (July 2004). "More lawyers than programmers". *Communications of the ACM*, 47(7).

Daim, T.U.; Rueda, G.; Martin, H.; & Gerdsri, P. (October 2006). "Forecasting emerging technologies: Use of bibliometrics and patent analysis". *Technological Forecasting and Social Change*, 73(8), pp.981-1012.

Davis, M. (1983). *Game theory: A Nontechnical introduction.* Mineola, NY: Dover Publications.

DeMarco, T. (1997). *The Deadline: A Novel about project management.* New York: Dorset House.

Denning, P. & Hayes-Roth, R. (November 2006). "Decision making in very large networks". *Communications of the ACM*, 49(11).

Department of Defense. (March 17, 2004). "Transformation Trends". http://www.oft.osd.mil/library/library_files/trends_346_Transformation%20Trends-11%20March%20%202004%20Issue-Version%20II.pdf

Drucker, P. (Jan-Feb 1967). "The Effective decision". *Harvard Business Review.*

Earl, M., & Feeny, D. (Spring, 1994). "Is your CIO adding value?" *Sloan Management Review*, 35(3), pp. 11-23.

Earl, M., & Feeny, D. (Winter 2000). "Opinion: How to be a CEO for the information age". *Sloan Management Review*, 41(2), pp. 11-23.

Eisenhardt, K. (September 1989). "Making fast strategic decisions in high-velocity environments". *Academy of Management Journal*, 32(3).

Elliott, L. (April 2000). "FEA in Y2K". *Desktop Engineering* online. http://www.deskeng.com/articles/00/Apr/feay2k2/main.htm

Eng, P. (August 21, 2004). "A Play for better soldiers". ABCnews.com. http://abcnews.go.com/sections/scitech/DailyNews/wargames 020821.html

Erickson, T.J., Magee, J.F., Roussel, P.A., & Saad, K.N. (1990). "Managing technology as a business strategy". *Sloan Management Review*, 31(3), p. 73.

Etzioni, A. (Jul-Aug 1989). "Humble decision making". *Harvard Business Review.*

Fayol, H. (1916). *General and industrial management.* London: Pittman Publishing.

Fishwick, P. (1995). *Simulation Model Design and Execution: Building digital worlds.* Englewood Cliffs, NJ: Principle Hall.

Ford, A. (1999). *Modeling the environment: An Introduction to system dynamics modeling of environmental systems*. Washington DC: Island Press.

Forrester, J.W. (Winter 2003). "Dynamic models of economic systems and industrial organizations". *System Dynamics Review*, 19(4), pp.329-345. (Reprint of Forrester's Research Notes from November 5, 1956).

Foster, R.N. (January-February, 2000). "Managing technological innovation for the next 25 years". *Research Technology Management*, 43(1), pp. 29-31.

Frank, R. (August 24, 2001). "Mary Doyle Named VP for WSU Information Technology". *WSU Today*.
http://www.wsu.edu/nis/doyle_m.html

French, J. & Raven, B. (1960). "The Bases of social power". In D. Cartwright & A. Zander (eds.), *Group dynamics* (pp. 607-623). New York: Harper and Row.

Frick, K.A., & Torres, A. (2002). "Learning from high-tech deals". *The McKinsey Quarterly*, 2002(1).

Fuchs, P., Mifflin, K., Miller, D. & Whitney, J. (Spring 2000). "Strategic integration: Competing in the age of capabilities", *California Management Review*, 42(3), pp. 107-129.

George, M., Works, J., & Watson-Hemphill, K. 2005. *Fast Innovation: Achieving superior differentiation, speed to market, and increased profitability*. New York: McGraw Hill.

Gibbons, S. (March/April 2000). "Down to a system: Keeping employee morale and retention high". *Journal for Quality and Participation*.

Gibson, R. (1998). *Rethinking the Future*. London: Nicholas Brealey Publishing.

Gladwell, M. (2005). *Blink: The Power of thinking without thinking*. New York: Little, Brown & Co.

Gonzalez, X. & Pazo, C. (January 15, 2004). "Firms' R&D dilemma: to undertake or not to undertake R&D". *Applied Economics Letters*, 11(1), 55-59.

Grundy, T. (October 2005). "Strategic decision-making". *Financial Management.*

Gwynne, P. (March-April, 1996). "The CTO as line manager". *Research Technology Management,* 39(2), pp. 14-19.

Hamel, G. & Prahalad, C. (1994) *Competing for the future,* Boston, MA: Harvard Business School Press.

Hammond, J.S.; Keeney, R.L.; & Raiffa, H. (Sept-Oct 1998). "The Hidden traps in decision making". *Harvard Business Review.*

Hammond, J.S.; Keeney, R.L.; Raiffa, H. (Mar-Apr 1998). "Even swaps: A Rational method for making trade-offs". *Harvard Business Review.*

Hampden-Turner, C. & Trompenaars, F. (2000). *Building cross-cultural competence: How to create wealth from conflicting values.* New Haven, CT: Yale University Press.

Hanson, D. (January 11, 2003). "Dr. Melodie Mayberry-Stewart City of Cleveland CTO at the GCPCUG Meeting". *Magnum Computers.* http://www.magnuminc.com/clevcto.htm

Hargadon, A. (2003). *How breakthroughs happen: The Surprising trust about how companies innovate.* Boston, MA: Harvard Business School Press.

Hari, P. (November 10, 2003). "We Use a Distributed R&D Model". *Businessworld* Online. http://www.businessworldindia.com/Nov1003/news13.asp

Harris, S. (January 18, 2002). "New federal CTO lays out his strategy". *GovExec.com.* http://governmentexecutive.com/dailyfed/0102/011802h1.htm

Hayashi, A.M. (Feb 2001). "When to trust your gut". *Harvard Business Review.*

Hof, R. (August 17, 2003). "Andy Grove: We can't even glimpse the potential". *Business Week* Online. http://www.businessweek.com/@@GovuBoUQaQmEPwkA/magazine/content/03_34/b3846612.htm

Homer, J. & Oliva, R. (Winter 2001). "Maps and models in system dynamics: A response to Coyle". *System Dynamics Review*, 17(4), pp.347-355.

Huebner, J. (October 2005). "A Possible declining trend for worldwide innovation". *Technological Forecasting & Social Change*, 72(8), pp.980-986. *Innovation*.

Jacobs, M. (June 2004). "Mary Doyle: Interim Director for WSU Libraries". Library news.
http://www.wsulibs.wsu.edu/LibWire/winter2000/doyle1200.html

Janis, I.L. (1989) *Crucial decisions: Leadership in policymaking and crisis management*. New York: The Free Press.

Jennings, D. & Wattman, S. (1998). *Decision making: An Integrated approach*. London: Pitman Publishing.

Kennedy, H. (November 2002). "Computer games liven up military recruiting , training". National Defense Magazine.
http://www.nationaldefensemagazine.org/article.cfm?Id=967

Ketchen, D; Snow, C.; Street, V. (November 2004). "Improving firm performance by matching strategic decision-making processes to competitive dynamics". *Academy of Management Executive*, 18(4).

Kimber, T. (2005). Professor's web site at State University of New York.
http://people.morrisville.edu/~kimbert/beta_mws/pois17.gif

Kripalani, M & Engardio, P. (December 8, 2003). "The Rise of India". *Business Week* online.

Kurtz, R. (June 2004). "Testing Testing ...". *Inc. Magazine*.

Kwak, M. (Spring 2001). "Technical skills, people skills, it's not either/or". *Sloan Management Review*, 41(3), p. 16.

Lane, D. (May 1995). "On a Resurgence of management simulations and games". *Journal of the Operational Research Society*, 46(5), pp. 604-625.

Larson, C. & Whiteley, R. (January-February, 2001). "Industrial Research Institute's 2nd annual R&D leaderboard: R&D spending by the top 100 U.S. technology investors in 1999". *Research Technology Management*,

44(1), 22-24.

Larson, C. (November, 2001). "Management for the new millennium–the challenge of change". *Research Technology Management,* 44(6), p. 10.

Law, A. & Kelton, W.D. (1991). *Simulation modeling and analysis.* New York: McGraw-Hill Publishers.

Lebbon, T. (2004). "Technology Valuations—The Whys and Wherefores and Why Nots". Leadenhall Australia Limited. [Online] Available: http://www.leadenhall.com.au/

Leifer, R, et.al. (2000). *Radical innovation: How mature companies can outsmart upstarts.* Boston, MA: Harvard Business School Press.

Leonard-Barton, D. (Summer 1992). "Core capabilities and core rigidities: A Paradox in new product development", *Strategic Management Journal,* 13, pp. 111-126.

Leslie, K.J., & Michaels, M.P. (2000). "The real power of real options". *The McKinsey Quarterly,* 3, 4-23.

Levitt, B. & March, J.G. "Organizational Learning". *Annual Review of Sociology* 14, pp. 319–340, 1998.

Lewis, W.W., & Lawrence, H.L. (1990). "A new mission for corporate technology". *Sloan Management Review,* 31(4), pp. 57-67.

Linstone, H.A. (1999). *Decision making for technology executives: Using multiple perspectives to improve performance.* Boston, MA: Artech House.

Lohr, S. (May 24, 2004). "The Distributor vs. the Innovator". *New York Times* online. http://query.nytimes.com/gst/abstract.html?res=F60713F63D5A0C7 78EDDAC0894DC404482

MacDonald, B.; Potter, J.M.; & Jensen, K.O. (April 2003). "Long-term business modeling using system dynamics". *BT Technology Journal,* 21(2), pp.158-170.

MacMillan, I.C.; van Putten, A.B.; McGrath, R.G.; & Thompson, J.D. (January-February 2006). "Using real options discipline for highly uncertain technology investments". *Research-Technology Management*, 49(1), 29-37.

Macrae, N. (1992). *John von Neumann: The Scientific genius who pioneered the modern computer, game theory, nuclear deterrence, and much more.* New York: Pantheon Books.

Mandelbrot, B. & Hudson, R. (2004). *The (Mis)Behavior of Markets.* Basic Books: New York.

Markides, C. & Geroski, P. 2005. *Fast second: How smart companies bypass radical innovation to enter and dominate new markets.* San Francisco, CA: Jossey-Bass.

Markides, C. 2002. "Strategic Innovation". *Innovation: Driving product, process, and market change.* Edited by E. Roberts. San Francisco, CA: Jossey-Bass.

McBride, S. (June 10, 2004). "Army 'Warrior' videogame is a hit with civilians too". Wall Street Journal.
http://confs.itcenter.org/listprocmil/attachments/MSG_26429_A.htm

McKnight, D. (January, 2002). The role of the CTO at Titan Corporation. Personal correspondence with the author.

McLaughlin, M. (April 19, 2004). "Robert Otto – Postal Service: Early to rise". *Government Computer News.* http://www.gcn.com/23_8/mgmt_edition/25546-1.html

Media Lab. (2001). Overview of the MIT Media Lab.
http://www.media.mit.edu/.

Metcalfe, R. (June 2004). "Why IT matters". *Technology Review.*
http://www.technologyreview.com/articles/04/06/metcalfe0604.asp?p=1

Miller, J. (April 7, 2003). "CTOs emerge as IT hubs for agencies". *Government Computer News.*
http://www.gcn.com/22_7/news/21600-1.html

Mintzberg, H. (Fall 1994). "Rounding out the manager's job". *Sloan Management Review*, pp.11-27.

Mintzberg, H. (Jan-Feb 1981). "Organization design: Fashion or fit?" *Harvard Business Review*.

Mintzberg, H. (Jan-Feb 1994). "The Fall and rise of strategic planning". *Harvard Business Review*.

Mintzberg, H. (Jul-Aug 1987). "Crafting strategy". *Harvard Business Review*.

Mintzberg, H. (Nov-Dec 2001). "Managing exceptionally". *Organization Science*, 12(6), pp.759-771.

Moder, J. & Elmaghraby, S. (1978). *Handbook of operations research: Foundations and fundamentals*. New York: Van Nostrand Reinhold.

Moore, G. (2005). *Dealing with Darwin: How great companies innovate at every phase of their evolution*. New York: Portfolio Books.

Morse, P. & Kimball, G. (1998). *Methods of operations research*. Alexandria, VA: Military Operations Research Society. (reprinted from the original 1951 manuscript)

Morton, S., et al. (2006). "The Role of social relationships in improving product development decision making". *Journal of Engineering Manufacture*, 220.

Mosquera, M. (September 8, 2003). "Veterans Affairs CTO Perry Retires". *Government Computer News*.
http://www.gcn.com/vol1_no1/daily-updates/23444-1.html

MSPCC. (not dated). "Biography of Michael Macedonia". Modeling and Simulation Professional Certification Commission web site.
http://www.simprofessional.org/about/Macedonia.html

National Academies. (not dated). "Aeronautics and Space Engineering Board: Dr. Malcolm R. O'Neill". National Academies web site.

National Research Council. (2006). "Defense modeling, simulation, and analysis". Washington D.C.: National Academies Press.
http://newton.nap.edu/catalog/11726.html

Newell, M.W. (2002). *Preparing for the Project Management Professional Certification Exam*. New York: AMACOM.

Nicholls, M.G.; Cargill, B.J.; & Dhir, K.S. (May 2004). "Using OR for diagnosis and facilitation in change programmes: a university application". *Journal of the Operational Research Society*, 55(5), pp.440-452.

Nutt, P. (March-April 1998). "Framing strategic decisions". *Organization Science*, 9(2).

O'Neill, P.H., & Bridenbaugh, P.R. (November-December, 1992). Credibility between CEO and CTO – A CEO's perspective; Credibility between CEO and CTO – A CTO perspective. *Research Technology Management*, 35(6), pp. 25-34.

OneCleveland. (2004). "OneCleveland Mission and Purpose".
http://www.onecleveland.com/

Open Group. (April 10, 2004). "Q&A with Dawn Meyerricks: Standards and Certification are Critical". The Open Group.
http://www.opengroup.org/comm/interviews/meyerriecks.htm

Orielle Inc. (2004). Management Team.
http://www.orielle.com/management/management.htm#bergman

Papadopoulos, Greg. (September 12, 2003). "Sun's Papadopoulos, Joy's Replacement, Looks Ahead".
http://today.java.net/pub/n/Papadopoulos_Looks_Ahead

Parker, D.P. (2002). «The Changing role of the Chief Technology Officer». D.P. Parker and Associates web site.
http://www.dpparker.com/article_cto_role.html.

Perelman, M. (Summer 1995). «Retrospectives: Schumpeter, David Wells, and Creative Destruction». *Journal of Economic Perspectives*, 9(3), 189-197.

Petura, B. (December 16, 2002). "Mary Doyle Appointed to Dual Administrative Roles". WSU News.
http://wsunews.wsu.edu/detail.asp?StoryID=3507

Phair, M., & Rubin, D.K. (October 26, 1998). "Bytes, bucks and big pictures". *Engineering News Review*, 241(16), p. 29.

Porter, M. (1985). *Competitive Advantage: Creating and sustaining superior performance,* New York: The Free Press.

Postrel, V. (June 27, 2004). "Operation everything". *Boston Globe* newspaper. http://www.dynamist.com/articles-speeches/opeds/opresearch.html

Prahalad, C. (May-June, 1998). "Managing discontinuities: The Emerging challenges", *Research Technology Management*, 41(3), pp. 14-22.

Prahalad, C. & Hamel, G. (May-June 1990). "The Core competence of the corporation". *Harvard Business Review*, 68(3), pp.79-91.

Rajagopalan, N; Rasheed, A.; Datta, D. (Summer 1993). "Strategic decision processes: Critical review and future directions". *Journal of Management*, 19(2).

Rich, B. & Janos, L. (1996). *Skunk Works*. Little, Brown & Company.

Robb, W.L. (September-October, 1994). "Selling technology to your CEO". *Research Technology Management*, 37(5), pp. 43-45.

Roberts, E. (March-April, 2001). "Benchmarking global strategic management of technology". *Research Technology Management*, 44(2), pp. 25-36.

Robinson, J. & Godbey, G. (Summer 2005). "Busyness as usual". *Social Research*, 72(2).

Rogers, E. (1962). *Diffusion of Innovations*. New York: Simon & Schuster.

Russell, S. & Norvig, P. (1995). *Artificial intelligence: A Modern approach*. New York: Prentice Hall.

Sauter, V. (June 1999). "Intuitive decision-making". *Communications of the ACM*, 42(6).

Scannell, E. (February 2, 2004). "IBM's Grady Booch on Solving Complexity". *InfoWorld* Magazine. p.15.

Schmitz, B. (December 2001). "CFD: Not Just of ExpertsAnymore". *Desktop Engineering* online. http://www.deskeng.com/articles/01/dec/feature1/main.htm

Schumpeter, J.A. (1942). *Capitalism, Socialism, and Democracy*. New York: Harper & Brothers.

Senge, P.M. (1990). *The Fifth discipline: The Art and practice of the learning organization.* New York: Doubleday Press.

Sharif, N. (1995). "The Evolution of technology management studies: Technoeconomics to technometrics", *Technology management: Strategies and applications for practitioners,* 2(3), pp. 113-148.

Sharif, N. (1999). "Strategic role of technological self-reliance in development management", *Technological forecasting and social change,* 44(1), pp. 219-238.

Shoemaker, P. (January 1993). "Strategic decisions in organizations: Rational and behavioral views". *Journal of Management,* 30(1).

Smith, D. & Alexander, R. (1999). *Fumbling the future: How Xerox invented then ignored the first personal computer.* New York: HarperCollins.

Smith, R. (July-August, 2003). "The Chief Technology Officer: Strategic Responsibilities and Relationships". *Research-Technology Management.*

Spiers, D. (July 5, 2001). "CTOs: Technology's easy—It's the people part that's hard to master". *Business 2.0,* pp.15-16.

Spinney, J. (July 1997). "Ghengis John". *Proceedings of the U.S. Naval Institute.* http://www.d-n-i.net/fcs/comments/c199.htm.

Stalk, G., Evans, P. & Shulman, L. (March-April, 1992). "Competing on capabilities: The New rules of corporate strategy", *Harvard Business Review,* 70(2), pp. 57-69.

Standard & Poor's. (2005). COMPUSTAT Database web site. http://www.compustat.com/www/db/me_lev3_01_db.html

Stave, K.A. (Summer 2002). "Using system dynamics to improve public participation in environmental decisions". *System Dynamics Review,* 18(2), pp.139-158.

Sterman, J. (2000). *Business Dynamics: Systems Thinking and Modeling for a Complex World.* McGraw Hill. New York: NY.

Stryker, P. (Jul-Aug 1965). "How to analyze that problem: Part II of a management exercise". *Harvard Business Review.*

Stryker, P. (May-Jun 1965). "Can you analyze this problem?" *Harvard Business Review.*

Subramaniam, M. & Youndt, M. June 2005. "The Influence of intellectual capital on the types of innovative capabilities". Academy of Management Journal, 48(3), 450-463. *System Dynamics*

Szewczyk, S.; Tsetsekos, G.; & Zantout, Z. (Spring 1996). "The valuation of corporate R&D expenditures: Evidence from investment opportunities and free cash flow". *Financial Management,* 25(2), 105-110.

Taylor, F.W. (1911). *The Principles of scientific management.* Mineola, NY: Dover Publishing (1998 edition).

Teece, D., Pisano, G., & Shuen, A. (2001). "Dynamic capabilities and strategic management", in *Nature & Dynamics of Organizational Capabilities,* Oxford University Press.

Thomke, S. (2003). *Experimentation matters: Unlocking the potential of new technologies for innovation.* Boston, MA: Harvard Business School Press.

Thurlings, B., & Debackere, K. (July-August, 1996). "Trends in managing industrial innovation—first insights from a field survey". *Research Technology Management,* 39(4), pp. 13-14.

Useem, M. (Summer 2003). "Corporate governance is directors making decisions: Reforming the outward foundations for inside decision making". *Journal of Management and Governance,* 7(3), pp.241-255.

Useem, M. & Cook, J. (Fall 2005). "Developing leaders for decision making under stress: Wildland firefighters in he South Canyon fire and its aftermath". *Academy of Management Learning and Education,* 4(4).

Utterback, J. (1996). *Mastering the dynamics of innovation.* Boston, MA: Harvard Business School Press.

Van Putten, A. & MacMillan, I. (December 2004). "Making real options really work". *Harvard Business Review,* 82(12), 134-141.

Varon, E. (October 1, 2002). "Who made IT happen?" *CIO Magazine.* http://www.cio.com/archive/100102/honoree_inv_meyerriecks.html

Virginia Piedmont Technology Council. (2004). Tech Awards 2004.
http://www.vptc.org/techawards/

von Hippel, E. (2005). *Democratizing innovation*. Boston, MA: MIT Press.

von Hippel, E. (Summer 2001). "Innovation by user communities: Learning from open-source software". *MIT Sloan Management Review*.

Waite, W. (January, 2002). The role of the CTO at Aegis Technologies. Personal correspondence with the author.

Washington State University. (2004). Biography of Mary Doyle.
http://infotech.wsu.edu/vpis/

Wheelwright, S.C. & Makridakis, S. (1985). *Forecasting methods for management*. New York: John Wiley & Sons.

Whitehead, A.N. (1925). *Science and the modern world*. New York: Mentor Books.

Whiteley, R. & Larson, C. (January-February, 2000). "Industrial Research Institute's First annual R&D leaderboard: R&D spending by the top 100 U.S. technology investors in 1998". *Research Technology Management*, 43(1), 25-27.

Whiteley, R. (November-December, 2005). "Industrial Research Institute's 7th annual R&D leaderboard: R&D spending by the top 100 U.S. technology investors in 2004". *Research Technology Management*, 48(6), 13-18.

Yellig, J. (April 16, 2004). "Innovation Feted at Tech Awards". *The Daily Progress*.
http://www.dailyprogress.com/servlet/Satellite?pagename=CDP%2FMG
Article%2FCDP_BasicArticle&c=MGArticle&cid=1031774914407&path=

Youndt, M.; Subramaniam, M; & Snell, S. (March, 2004). "Intellectual capital profiles: An examination of investments and returns". *Journal of Management Studies*, 41(2), 335-361.

Zeltzer, D. (January, 2002). The role of the CTO at the Fraunhofer Institute. Personal correspondence with the author.

Dr. Smith provides consulting services around the effective practices of the CTO and Technology Executive. This includes a workshop on the *Top 10 Problems Faced by the CTO*. Contact us for additional information.

LaVergne, TN USA
29 November 2010
206549LV00003B/23/P